Laaibah
W9-APF-886

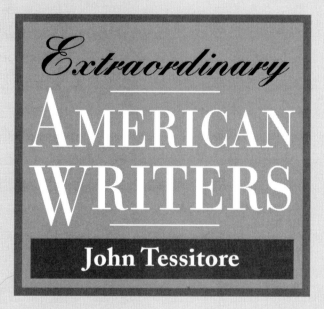

Extraordinary

AMERICAN WRITERS

John Tessitore

Children's Press®
A Division of Scholastic Inc.
New York Toronto London Auckland Sydney
Mexico City New Delhi Hong Kong
Danbury, Connecticut

Interior design by Elizabeth Helmetsie

Library of Congress Cataloging-in-Publication Data

Tessitore, John.
    Extraordinary American writers / John Tessitore
        p. cm.
    Summary: Profiles more than sixty United States authors representing different eras,
cultures, and genres who made their mark in history, including Benjamin Franklin, Emily
Dickinson, and W. E. B. Du Bois.
    Includes bibliographical references and index.
    ISBN 0-516-22656-8
    1. Authors, American—Biography—Juvenile literature. [1. Authors, American.] I. Title.

PS129.T47 2004
810.9—dc21
              2003004445

©2004 Children's Press, a Division of Scholastic Inc.
All rights reserved. Published simultaneously in Canada.
Printed in the United States of America.

For my son Nicholas, an extraordinary person.

Contents

50

Edgar Allan Poe
1809–1849
Editor, Poet, Master
of the Short Story

66

Herman Melville
1819–1891
Writer of Complex
Novels, Including
Moby-Dick

82

Louisa May Alcott
1832–1888
Children's Author,
Social Reformer

54

Harriet Beecher Stowe
1811–1896
Author of
Antislavery Novel
Uncle Tom's Cabin

72

Susan Warner
1819–1885
Best-Selling Writer
of Sentimental Fiction

86

Horatio Alger
1832–1899
Novelist Best Known
for Rags-to-Riches
Stories

58

Frederick Douglass
1817(?)–1895
Escaped Slave,
Leading Abolitionist

75

Walt Whitman
1819–1892
Poet of American
Democracy

89

Mark Twain
1835–1910
Humorist, Satirist,
Celebrated Novelist

62

Henry David Thoreau
1817–1862
Transcendental
Essayist, Nature Writer

79

Emily Dickinson
1830–1886
Poet of Personal
Spirituality

94

William Dean Howells
1837–1920
Realist Novelist,
Influential Editor

98

Henry James
1843–1916
Writer of Psychological
Novels and Short
Stories

114

Edith Wharton
1862–1937
Novelist of New
York's High Society

129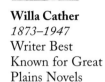

Willa Cather
1873–1947
Writer Best
Known for Great
Plains Novels

102

Kate Chopin
1851–1904
Feminist Writer
Best Known for
The Awakening

118

W.E.B. Du Bois
1868–1963
Civil Rights
Activist, Historian,
Social Theorist

133

Robert Frost
1874–1963
Poet of Rural
New England

105

Booker T. Washington
1856–1915
African American
Educator, Memoirist

122

Stephen Crane
1871–1900
Realist Novelist,
Wartime Reporter

138

Gertrude Stein
1874–1946
Experimental Writer,
Patron of the Arts

109

Owen Wister
1860–1938
Creator of the
Modern Western

125

Theodore Dreiser
1871–1945
Naturalist Novelist,
Social Critic

142

Jack London
1876–1916
Writer of Popular
Adventure Stories

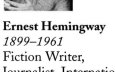

194

Langston Hughes
1902–1967
Jazz Poet of the
Harlem Renaissance

210

Tennessee Williams
1911–1983
Southern Playwright,
Theatrical Innovator

227

Robert Lowell
1917–1977
Confessional Poet of
New England Society

198

John Steinbeck
1902–1968
Writer Best Known for
Depression-Era Fiction

215

Ralph Ellison
1914–1994
Writer Best Known
for *Invisible Man*

231

J. D. Salinger
1919–
Reclusive Author of
The Catcher in the Rye

202

Richard Wright
1908–1960
Protest Novelist,
Champion of
Racial Equality

219

Saul Bellow
1915–
Novelist of Modern
American Anxiety

234

Jack Kerouac
1922–1969
Novelist,
Spokesman of the
Beat Generation

206

Eudora Welty
1909–2001
Writer of the
Deep South

223

Arthur Miller
1915–
Popular Playwright
Best Known for
Death of a Salesman

238

Kurt Vonnegut
1922–
Popular Satirist of
Modern America

Introduction

The United States has an exceptionally rich literary history despite its relative youth among the nations of the world. Its basic institutions—its system of government, its constitutional protection of the freedom of speech, its tradition of public education, its extensive networks of newspapers and magazines—all encourage a population of readers and writers. As a result, there are hundreds of literary figures, past and present, who qualify for a book entitled *Extraordinary American Writers*. The writers depicted on the following pages are the ones you are likely to encounter in your studies, the ones who occupy central positions in classes about American literature and history.

For the most part, they are writers who examined and analyzed American society in their works, who considered the nation as a whole in addition to their more personal concerns. That is why this book begins with Benjamin Franklin, the oldest of the Founding Fathers, and not with some of the other exceptional writers whose works were published during the colonial era, before the creation of the United States. *Extraordinary American Writers* ultimately traces the role writers have played, from the nation's birth to the present era, in defining America's unique culture.

It also provides a broad survey of American literary history through the biographies of men and women who expressed themselves through a range of genres, including novels, short stories, plays, poetry, and essays. Many genres are still missing; this book does not present the lives of full-time journalists, orators, politicians, or even many philosophers, though Ralph Waldo Emerson and Henry David Thoreau certainly fall into this last category. Rather, it includes the stories of men and women who believed themselves to be writers above all else, who valued the act of combining words on a page more than any of their secondary functions as philosophers, scholars, or critics. This is a book about people who changed the way other people learned to read and write.

It is also a book of life stories, however, and some lives make better stories than others. Writers are usually judged by their work, not their actions. They spend hours alone, at their desks, pouring through dictionaries and thesauri to find the right words to express their ideas. Often, such lives make for colorless biographies. Nevertheless, some writers do lead fascinating and exciting lives: Susanna Rowson was both a leading actress and an education reformer in the years after the Revolution; Frederick Douglass escaped slavery to become one of the most influential public figures of his age; Herman Melville spent three years exploring the South Pacific as a sailor. For every Edgar Allan Poe, who wrote exciting stories but devoted his life to quieter, more literary endeavors, there is an Ernest Hemingway, who participated in three wars and sought adventure at all costs. But while this book contains many interesting life stories, it is designed to highlight the importance of the writers to American cultural history overall.

The act of writing has allowed a diverse array of people to achieve prominence in American society: writers from wealthy families, like James Fenimore Cooper, and from poor families, like Raymond Carver; writers from established families, like Robert Lowell, and from immigrant families, like Saul Bellow; writers from African American families, like Toni Morrison; writers from the South, like Eudora Welty; writers from the Midwest, like Willa Cather. Studied together, these men and women present a complicated portrait of American society. Their biographies, like their works, are not simple stories. They are the biographies of people who experienced and studied the world around them, and they are as complicated as that world has proven to be. Hopefully, this book will inspire you to seek out more information about them and their beautiful, challenging, and important works.

Benjamin Franklin

Statesman, Scientist, Inventor, Writer
1706–1790

Benjamin Franklin was arguably the most important American of his vitally important era. As a statesman, he helped to lead the American Revolution, helped to draft the Declaration of Independence and the Constitution, and won support for the United States government abroad. As a scientist, he made several important discoveries about the natural world. As an inventor, he designed machines that improved the quality of everyday life. And as a writer, he did more than any other Founding Father to define the American character.

Franklin was born on January 17, 1706, the fifteenth of seventeen children in the family of Josiah Franklin, a candle maker, in Boston. At thirteen years of age, he was apprenticed to his brother James, a printer. This arrangement proved an unhappy one for Benjamin, however. Although he attracted some notice for the witty articles he published in his brother's newspaper, and although he proved adept at running the newspaper during his brother's occasional absences, young Benjamin suffered his brother's harsh words and rough treatment. So, in 1723, the seventeen-year-old printer and writer fled his family and set off alone for Philadelphia.

Though friendless when he arrived, Franklin quickly attracted supporters in his adopted city, including the British governor of the Pennsylvania colony, Sir William Keith. Soon he was planning to print his own Philadelphia newspaper. With Keith's encouragement and a promise of financial support, Franklin sailed to London to purchase a printing press. But Keith never sent the money he promised, and Franklin found himself stuck in London, friendless again.

Charming and resourceful, he found employment in two of the larger printing houses in London and was able to save enough money to return to

> If time be of all Things the most precious, *wasting Time* must be, as *Poor Richard* says, *the greatest Prodigality*, since, as he elsewhere tells us, *Lost Time is never found again;* and what we call *Time-enough*, *always proves little enough.*
>
> ~ *Poor Richard's Almanack*

Philadelphia in 1728 and start his own business. For the next twenty years, he would print official government documents, newspapers, and most famously, *Poor Richard's Almanack,* an annual compendium of information for farmers that also included Franklin's own witty advice for good living. His plainspoken character, Poor Richard, was among the first distinctly American figures in colonial literature; Richard's straightforward wisdom, and particularly his celebration of hard work, suggested that the colonists were developing a way of thinking (and writing) that set them apart from their British cousins.

While managing his printing firm, Franklin participated in the life of the city. He worked in the colonial legislature, was appointed deputy postmaster of the colonies, and organized the first fire company in Philadelphia. He also founded the first circulating library in the colonies, supported public construction projects, convened the American Philosophical Society, organized the first colonial hospital, and inspired the creation of the University of Pennsylvania. By 1748 these and other projects increasingly occupied his time and energy, and because he had already accumulated enough wealth to support his family for the rest of his life, he retired from the printing business. Only forty-two years old, Franklin had already amassed an impressive list of achievements. And he had not yet begun his scientific or political careers in earnest.

In the late 1740s, he began to experiment on the poorly understood phenomenon of electricity. He was interested in other scientific matters, such as the causes of earthquakes, and invented several new devices including the lightning rod and bifocal eyeglasses, but electricity was the subject of his most important discoveries. Most famously, in his kite experiment of 1752—which others attempted first, following his suggestions—he proved the relationship between electricity and lightning. He published the results of these and other experiments in *Experiments and Observations on Electricity*

(1751–53), on the strength of which he became an internationally acclaimed scientific figure.

By the beginning of the Revolutionary War, Franklin had also become one of the most famous politicians in North America. He had been elected to the Pennsylvania Assembly, had served as deputy postmaster of the British colonies, and had been one of the most outspoken colonial leaders during the French and Indian War. Beginning in the mid-1760s he served as a colonial delegate to the Crown during the initial conflicts that led to the Revolution. Though a loyal subject of the British king for most of his life, he found it difficult to maintain his allegiance as the conflict intensified in the mid-1770s. By the time he left London and returned to Philadelphia in 1775, the war was already on, and Franklin decided to support the revolutionaries. He accepted a post in the Second Continental Congress, where he provided guidance to the younger delegates, including Thomas Jefferson as he wrote the Declaration of Independence. Capitalizing on his fame in Europe, the Congress then appointed him its delegate to France, where he secured the support of the French king for the colonial army, a diplomatic victory that helped ensure American independence. In 1783, he was one of the delegates who signed the Treaty of Paris, ending the war.

Returning to the United States in 1785, he served on the Pennsylvania executive council, attended the Constitutional Convention in 1787, and founded one of the nation's first antislavery societies, the Pennsylvania Abolition Society. These final acts of service concluded a life of exceptional achievement. Franklin died on April 17, 1790.

But his greatest literary achievement was still to come. In 1868, seventy-eight years after his death, Franklin's *Autobiography* was published in its entirety for the first time. Begun as a family history written for one of his sons, the autobiography traces Franklin's progress from childhood through his early successes in the Pennsylvania colony. One of the first portrayals of the American self-made man—a person from humble origins who achieves fame and wealth in a democratic society—it quickly became a standard text in American literature and has inspired many imitators. Displaying some of the wit and wisdom of Poor Richard and some of the intelligence and insight of the master statesman he had become, *Autobiography* is Franklin's clearest description of American character—its persistence and industriousness—a character he helped to create and one that he perfected in his own life.

Phillis Wheatley

African American Poet, Slave
1753(?)–1784

*P*hillis Wheatley was born in the western region of Africa near Senegal. Before her eighth birthday, she was kidnapped by slave traders, sent to Boston, Massachusetts, and sold into service in the house of John Wheatley, a wealthy tailor. Sickly, alone, and barely able to communicate with her English-speaking owners, she suffered untold hardships.

But Wheatley possessed talents that could not be denied, not even

> Still, wond'rous youth! each noble path pursue,
> On deathless glories fix thine ardent view:
> Still may the painter's and poet's fire
> To aid thy pencil, and thy verse conspire!
> And may the charms of each seraphic theme
> Conduct thy footsteps to immortal fame!
>
> ∼ From "To S.M., a Young African
> Painter, on Seeing His Works"

within the institution of slavery. And she enjoyed an unusual amount of support from the Wheatley family. As a result of their instruction, she became fluent in English within two years of her arrival and went on to attain a working knowledge of Latin and Greek.

Through her studies, she discovered the poetry of the English masters—John Milton and Alexander Pope—as well as the stories of the Bible, and she was soon writing verse of her own.

Wheatley published her first poem in 1767. With her 1770 elegy for George Whitefield, a famous preacher of the era, she earned the admiration of many New England writers and editors. Extraordinary among slaves for having been given the opportunity to show her work, she also proved exceptionally skillful at the evenly rhymed, spiritually uplifting style of poetry that was popular during the mid-1700s. Her dedication to the Harvard College class of 1767, "To the University of Cambridge, in New-England," became one of the most popular poems of the period. Though she frequently referred to her slave status in her poems, particularly in poems like "On Being Brought from Africa to America," she wrote most often about religious and inspirational matters and avoided the political controversies of the age.

In 1773, she accompanied the Wheatleys on a trip to London. In the capital of the British Empire, she was celebrated by politicians and nobles for her literary achievements. By proving that African slaves could be artists and intellectuals as well as laborers, Wheatley astonished European society. Still, book publishers in America were afraid to acknowledge her abilities and refused to publish her complete volume, *Poems on Various Subjects, Religious and Moral* (1773), which was ultimately accepted by a British firm.

Upon returning from England, the Wheatleys freed Phillis, but the poet continued to live with and work for the family. She also continued writing and earned the praise of George Washington for some of the poems she wrote during the Revolutionary era. In 1778, John Wheatley died, leaving Phillis to support herself. She married a free African American, John Peters, but neither was able to earn a living in Boston. Despite all of the recognition she had received, and despite her hard-earned freedom, Wheatley was still limited by American racial prejudice. She was forced to work as a seamstress and remained impoverished for the rest of her life. Her three children died in infancy, and Phillis herself died before she could complete her second volume of poems, in 1784.

Long before the antislavery struggle of the mid-nineteenth century, Phillis Wheatley proved that African Americans could participate in and advance American culture. Though not explicitly political, her poems were considered dangerous by some Americans; in their beauty and intelligence, they suggested that there was no justification for the ugly institution of slavery. Wheatley may not have enjoyed the full benefits of literary fame in her lifetime, but her work led the way for future African American writers, some of whom who would achieve both wealth and influence through their poetry.

Susanna Haswell Rowson

Best-Selling Novelist, Pioneer in Women's Education
1762–1824

In 1791, Susanna Haswell Rowson published *Charlotte: A Tale of Truth* (later renamed *Charlotte Temple*). The story of a fifteen-year-old English girl who accompanies her boyfriend to the American colonies, only to be mistreated and abandoned by him after they arrive, it became the best selling novel in America. And it continued to be a major cultural phenomenon through much of the nineteenth century. Many readers identified strongly with the title character. Some were so convinced that Rowson's novel was a true story that they laid flowers at a New York gravesite believed to be Charlotte's. But Rowson's own life story was even more amazing than that of her character. Living through dramatic political and social changes, she influenced American culture in important ways.

> 'I cannot think we have done exactly right in going out this evening, Mademoiselle,' said Charlotte, seating herself when she entered her apartment: 'nay, I am sure it was not right; for I expected to be very happy, but was sadly disappointed.'
>
> ~ From *Charlotte Temple*

The only child of William and Susanna Haswell, Rowson was born in Portsmouth, England, in 1762. Her mother died while giving birth to her, and her father, a lieutenant in the Royal Navy, accepted a post as a customs officer in the American colonies shortly thereafter. Young Susanna was raised by relatives until she joined her father in the Massachusetts colony in 1766. Surviving this tragic beginning, she had a relatively happy childhood, living among the powerful leaders of the British colonies. But with the coming of the American Revolution, everything changed. As the war began in 1775, her father, a British officer and supporter of King George III, found himself surrounded by enemies. Colonial leaders stripped the Haswell family of its property and made William a prisoner of war. In 1778 they forced him and his family to return to England.

Penniless but unbroken, Susanna soon took charge of her own life. Capitalizing on the fine education she received in the colonies, she embarked on a literary career. It was a rare choice for a woman of that era, but she proved to be a prolific, self-confident writer. In 1786 she published her first novel, *Victoria.* In the following years, she published several more, as well as two volumes of poetry. In 1791 she published the work that would make her famous, *Charlotte Temple.*

Though young readers typically responded to the plot twists and intrigue of the story, as well as to the sadness of the title character's decline, *Charlotte Temple* is a novel designed to instruct young girls about how to survive in a dangerous world. Rowson explicitly addressed her tale to impressionable girls searching for husbands and blinded by fairy-tale versions of love. By detailing Charlotte's hardships, she hoped to teach these girls to protect themselves from untrustworthy men. The tragedy of the novel is that Charlotte does not learn to protect herself until it is too late; Rowson hoped to save others from the same fate.

Unlike Charlotte, Susanna Haswell knew how to fend for herself by 1791. Not only did she recover from the decline of her family's fortune after the American Revolution, but she learned to cope with her own shiftless husband. She had married William Rowson, a military musician and owner of a hardware business, in 1786. But by the time Susanna published *Charlotte Temple,* it was clear that William was undependable, a burden more than a partner. When his hardware business failed in 1792, Susanna became the primary breadwinner in the Rowson home.

That year, she joined a theater company and led her family back to the United States. For the New Theater in Philadelphia, she wrote several plays and performed in a variety of leading roles. She also managed to write another novel, *Trials of the Human Heart.* Then, in 1796, she moved to Boston and acted in that city's Federal Street Theater.

Despite her theatrical successes, she left the stage for good a year later and returned to the occupation that interested her most, one that she first explored in *Charlotte Temple*: the education of young girls. In 1797 she opened the Young Ladies' Academy in Boston, which proved to be one of the finest women's educational institutions in the country. Rowson oversaw the daily operations of the school and was largely responsible for its curriculum. She wrote textbooks in spelling, geography, and world history that highlighted the roles of women in society and introduced her students to early feminist ideas.

By the time Susanna Haswell Rowson died, on March 2, 1824, she had mastered the popular arts of the age, advanced new educational and feminist theories, and produced the first best-seller in U.S. literary history. Understandably, *Charlotte Temple* would be the primary basis of her reputation. But even without that novel, Rowson was one of the most accomplished women of the early republic.

Charles Brockden Brown

Gothic Novelist, Social Critic
1771–1810

For many Americans, the Revolution represented an exciting break with the past, an opportunity to rebuild society according to new theories about individual rights and representation. But some Americans of the Revolutionary era, like novelist Charles Brockden Brown, experienced the war as a personal tragedy and were less optimistic about the young nation's future. Brown's novels—

among the first in American literature—offered a portrait of the United States that was very different from those presented by writers like Benjamin Franklin. In his best work, which explored political ideas through popular fiction, he warned Americans about the hidden dangers of their new society.

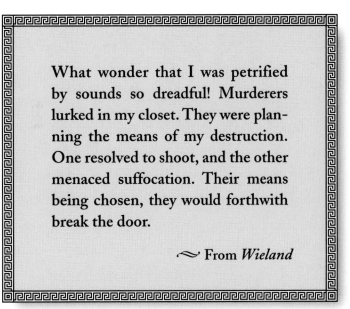

What wonder that I was petrified by sounds so dreadful! Murderers lurked in my closet. They were planning the means of my destruction. One resolved to shoot, and the other menaced suffocation. Their means being chosen, they would forthwith break the door.

∼ From *Wieland*

A Quaker and a pacifist, Brown's father refused to participate in the Revolution. By also failing to declare his allegiance, however, he made enemies on both sides of the war. In 1777 he was arrested for treason by the patriot army and exiled to Virginia. Young Charles Brockden Brown therefore experienced the war as a family tragedy and an unjust separation from his father, and he would view the nation critically for the rest of his life.

After the war, he attended the Friends Latin School in Philadelphia, then studied law. But Brown never became a practicing lawyer. Instead, he followed some of his friends into the nation's growing literary business and made a name for himself in its literary capital, New York City. He wrote essays for literary magazines, drafted several unpublished novels, and in 1798 published his first book-length work, an early analysis of feminism entitled *Alcuin*. In that same year, he wrote the four novels that would seal his reputation as a major voice in American literature.

Writing furiously in this period, he completed *Ormond*, a Gothic novel through which he explored his interests in social reform and women's rights; *Edgar Huntly*, noteworthy as an early fictional representation of Native Americans; half of *Arthur Mervyn*, describing the yellow-fever epidemic of 1793; and his masterpiece, *Wieland; or The Transformation*.

Set in rural Pennsylvania, *Wieland* is the story of the mild, cultured Wieland family, whose peace and happiness are disturbed when they begin to hear mysterious voices. Sometimes the voices of strangers, sometimes the voices of family members, and sometimes the voice of God, they begin to influence the Weilands' behavior. After a series of misunderstandings, culminating in a gruesome murder, the voices are revealed to be the work of a ventriloquist who intended to trick, but not to harm, the family. While the novel generates the excitement of popular murder mysteries and Gothic horror stories, Brown intended for it to be read as a political warning as well, a parable about deception and trickery in a democratic society, and a critique of the eloquent speakers who came to dominate American politics after the Revolution. He even sent a copy to Thomas Jefferson in the hope of influencing the future president's political decisions.

Following his extraordinarily productive year (1798–99), Brown wrote two more novels. Then he abandoned fiction completely, devoting more of his time to articles, essays, and translations. He also edited two journals, *The Monthly Magazine and American Review* and *The Literary Magazine and American Register*, before deciding that he could support his family only by changing careers and joining his brothers in their mercantile business. The brothers declared bankruptcy in 1806, however, and Brown returned to his writing desk. He penned a series of political pamphlets and essays and planned a book on geography before he died of tuberculosis in February 1810.

One of America's first novelists, and one of the first to make writing a full-time career, Brown anticipated many of the literary innovations of the nineteenth century. His philosophically rich Gothic tales influenced major American writers of the mid-1800s, including Edgar Allan Poe, Nathaniel Hawthorne, and Herman Melville. And his skepticism about American society in general, and about the Revolution in particular, resulted in some of the earliest and most thorough critiques of democracy in American literature.

Washington Irving

America's First Professional Writer

1783–1859

Early American writers did not earn a living by their pens alone. Typically they supported themselves through other jobs and wrote only in their spare time. With the publication of *The Sketch Book* in 1819, however, Washington Irving changed the way writers did business. *The Sketch Book* made Irving the first successful professional writer in the United States, as well as the first to earn the respect of European readers. More important, it introduced uniquely American subjects into popular literature and made Irving a central figure in early American culture.

Irving was born in New York City in 1783. His father was a wealthy Scottish immigrant who insisted that his five sons succeed in the business

> The chief part of the stories, however, turned upon the favorite spectre of Sleepy Hollow, the headless horseman, who had been heard several times of late, patrolling the country; and it was said, tethered his horse nightly among the graves in the church yard.
>
> ∾ From "The Legend of Sleepy Hollow"

world. Dutifully Washington studied law. But he disliked his profession and dreamed of a life devoted to literature. While still a student, he adopted the name "Jonathan Oldstyle" and wrote popular newspaper articles that ridiculed New York society. The success of these articles suggested that the nineteen-year-old Irving was well on his way to literary fame.

After completing his legal studies and then traveling through Europe, he returned to New York to half heartedly practice law and continue his literary pursuits. In 1807, with one of his brothers and his friend James Kirke Paulding, he published another set of satires, *Salmagundi,* and in 1809 he published the comic history *A History of New York, by Dietrich Knickerbocker.*

But Irving's blooming literary career was suddenly interrupted by tragedy: In 1809 his fiancée, Matilda Hoffman, died. Misfortune struck again when, shortly thereafter, one of the family businesses collapsed. Still in mourning and facing financial ruin, Irving was called to Washington, D.C., to help preserve the company his father had built.

In 1815, after devoting four years of his life to the business, Irving returned to Europe in the hope of regaining his literary form. Initially, writing was Irving's passion, the thing he loved to do and did well. But the sudden bankruptcy of the Irving importing firm in 1818 made writing a necessity. Without the financial security of his father's business, Irving was forced to rely on his literary imagination for his living. He therefore risked disaster by attempting what had seldom been accomplished by American writers: to live exclusively on the money earned by writing.

In 1819 he began publishing short articles and stories in major American and English magazines. No longer writing pure satires, Irving adapted fashionable styles to his own ideas. He wrote articles about travel, art appreciation, and American culture as well as short stories based on folk tales. The most famous and popular of these short pieces were two supernatural stories: "The Legend of Sleepy Hollow," about a young schoolteacher's encounter with a headless horseman, and "Rip Van Winkle," about a man who falls asleep during the colonial period of American history and wakes up years later, after the Revolution. Irving set both of these stories in New York State, thereby giving American readers, who were reading the works of English writers, their own literature.

Irving collected these stories into a volume entitled *The Sketch Book of Geoffrey Crayon, Gent.* It quickly became a critical and popular success. Surprisingly, it also secured his fortune, selling enough copies to support a comfortable lifestyle. Irving became a literary celebrity. In subsequent years he published several more volumes of fiction, including *Tales of a Traveller* (1824), as well as comic plays.

His celebrity also earned him a number of government appointments. He lived in Spain from 1826 to 1829 as a U.S. diplomat and from 1842 to 1845 as the U.S. minister to the Spanish government. He also worked as a diplomat in London from 1826 to 1831. During these periods, he continued to write stories like those found in his Spanish-influenced collection, *The Alhambra* (1832), and collected material for his important histories, including *A History in the Life and Voyages of Christopher Columbus* (1828).

Returning to the United States in 1832, he focused his attention on the American West in a series of stories and histories. Then, after declining several high-profile government positions—he was asked to run for Congress, to serve as mayor of New York, and to serve as secretary of the Navy—he began his best historical work, the five-volume *Life of George Washington*. Settling in Tarrytown, New York, the village he had renamed "Sleepy Hollow" in his famous story, Irving spent the rest of his life preparing his biography of the nation's first president. It was a fitting final effort for the writer who had done more than any other to create a literary tradition in the United States.

James Fenimore Cooper

Master of the American Action–Adventure Story
1789–1851

Stories about brave, crafty outdoorsmen have long dominated American popular culture. Even before there were cowboys roaming the Wild West, American literature was populated by scouts and hunters, men who roamed the mountains of the Northeast and lived free and independent lives. The writer most responsible for creating these literary figures, James Fenimore Cooper, was neither a wanderer nor an outdoorsman. But from the comfort of his estate in New York, he invented the characters on whom action and adventure heroes have been based ever since.

Cooper was born on September 15, 1789, in Burlington, New Jersey. His father, a wealthy and influential judge, moved his family to an estate—now known as the village of Cooperstown—in central New York the following year. Thus Cooper grew up in privilege and luxury, and unlike the heroes of his later fiction, he received a first-rate education. He was privately tutored and attended Yale University until he was expelled during his junior year, in 1805, for bad behavior. Certain that he could always rely on his family's fortune for survival but uncertain about his own place in the world, he spent the next six years at sea, including three years in the U.S. Navy. In 1811 he returned to Cooperstown, married Susan August DeLancey, the daughter of a wealthy New York landowner, and set to work managing the fortunes of both families.

In 1820 he wrote his first novel, an imitation of popular British novels called *Precaution*, largely to amuse himself and his wife. Recognizing its shortcomings but suddenly determined to achieve success as a writer, he devoted his second novel, 1821's *The Spy*, to a subject closer to his heart: the American Revolution. As an action-packed historical adventure, *The Spy* set Cooper on

> The form of Hawkeye had crouched like a beast about to take its spring, and his frame trembled so violently with eagerness, that the muzzle of the half-raised rifle played like a leaf fluttering in the wind.
>
> ⁓ From *The Last of the Mohicans*

the course he would master in the novel series he began with his third effort, *The Pioneers* (1823).

The Pioneers introduced American readers to Cooper's most famous hero, Natty Bumppo. Bumppo would appear in four more of Cooper's novels—*The Last of the Mohicans* (1826), *The Prairie* (1827), *The Pathfinder* (1840), and *The Deerslayer* (1841)—under a variety of names including "Deerslayer," "Hawkeye," "Pathfinder," and "Leatherstocking." A guide and scout for the British army before the Revolution and for the American army after the Revolution, he participates in the many conflicts between European settlers and Native Americans in New York. Fighting with honor and protecting settlers who do not share his survival skills, Bumppo never concerns himself with the accumulation of wealth or property. Instead, he and his loyal friend Chingachgook, a one-time chief of the Mohican tribe, help spread American society West, even as Bumppo remains a man of the wilderness.

As a selfless supporter of pioneers, Bumppo was an attractive character to Americans in the first half of the nineteenth century, when territorial expansion was the primary issue in American politics and few objected to the displacement of Native American tribes. Almost immediately, American writers began copying Cooper's tales, and Bumppo became the model for a variety of American action heroes, including the cowboys of the late-nineteenth and twentieth centuries.

In 1850 Cooper compiled all of the Bumppo novels into a uniform series, *The Leather-Stocking Tales.* By then he had also published several popular novels about the high seas, including 1823's *The Pilot,* and was known at home and abroad as the premier writer of American popular adventure. But Cooper's personal reputation was more complicated than his literary reputation, especially in the United States. Many distrusted him because of his status as a wealthy landowner; others objected to the fact that he lived in Europe from 1826 to 1833 and wrote critically about American culture as a result of his European experiences. At a time when America was becoming more democratic in its political and social structures, Cooper seemed to become more aristocratic, advocating a society based on wealth in works such as *A Letter to His Countrymen* (1834) and *The American Democrat* (1838). Even his later novels, including a trilogy known as the Littlepage Manuscripts—*Satanstoe* (1845), *The Chainbearer* (1845), and *The Redskins* (1846)—demonstrated his changing outlook on his native land. Abandoning the rugged outdoorsmen and heroic sailors of his earlier adventures, Cooper now wrote about landholding families in conflict with their tenants.

The late Cooper novels may have confused and angered some readers, but they did not diminish the overall popularity of his literary output. *The Leather-Stocking Tales* in particular earned Cooper a diverse and lasting audience. The most famous of those tales, *The Last of the Mohicans,* is still considered a classic, the subject of children's books and popular movies as well as a major novel in the history of American literature. Most important, in Natty Bumppo, James Fenimore Cooper created a new kind of hero—selfless, resourceful, virtuous—for a new kind of nation.

Ralph Waldo Emerson

Philosopher, Essayist, Leading Transcendentalist
1803–1882

At his home in Concord, Massachusetts, Ralph Waldo Emerson entertained the greatest American thinkers of the early nineteenth century. Essayist Henry David Thoreau, educator Bronson Alcott, editor and early feminist Margaret Fuller, novelist Nathaniel Hawthorne, and other writers and philosophers congregated at his house to share ideas and receive encouragement. This "Concord school" of intellectuals, otherwise known as the Transcendentalists, would help to create the first uniquely American philosophy. And Emerson, as the leader of this group, was the most influential transcendentalist of all.

Emerson was born in Boston on May 25, 1803, into a family of influential Protestant ministers. His grandfather was a pastor in Concord in the late 1700s and lived close to

> Trust thyself: every heart vibrates to that iron string. Accept the place the divine providence has found for you, the society of your contemporaries, the connection of events. Great men have always done so.
>
> ~ From "Self-Reliance"

the spot where British and colonial soldiers fired the first shots of the American Revolution. His father, William Emerson, was pastor of the First Unitarian Church of Boston. After William died in 1811, Emerson's mother struggled to support her five sons. Ralph Waldo received the education of an aspiring minister. He attended Harvard College and Harvard Divinity School, preparing to follow his father into the Unitarian pulpit.

In 1829, Emerson became pastor of the Second Unitarian Church of Boston, where he developed his unique preaching style. Writing was Emerson's true passion. He was less fond of his other clerical duties. By the time he was ordained he was already beginning to doubt some of the Unitarian teachings. When his young wife Ellen died of tuberculosis in 1831 (he would marry again in 1835), his life seemed in disarray. No longer satisfied with his church responsibilities and uncertain of his future, he resigned from Second Unitarian Church in 1832 and traveled to Europe.

In England he met poet and philosopher Samuel Taylor Coleridge, essayist

Thomas Carlyle, and Romantic poet William Wordsworth. In conversations with these men, Emerson began to sort out his own ideas. When he returned to the United States in 1834, he was ready to introduce his new philosophy, transcendentalism, to the world. Transcendentalism never featured a set of absolute laws; instead it emphasized certain important ideas: the power of the individual to change the world, the importance of self-reliance and independence for personal and community happiness, and the existence of God within every living person. Part religion, part philosophy, part literary theory, transcendentalism dominated northern American thought in the years before the Civil War.

Without an organized church for support, Emerson drew his income from the publication of his writings as well as from his frequent lecture tours. In an age before mass entertainment, Americans often paid to hear lectures by experts in the sciences and the arts. And for several decades, Emerson was among the nation's favorite speakers.

Emerson's first long essay, "Nature" (1836), laid the foundations of his thought and caused a small stir in intellectual circles. During the next two years, he scandalized Americans with two lectures delivered at Harvard: "The American Scholar" in 1837 and "The Divinity School Address" of 1838. In both of these lectures, Emerson criticized traditional ways of thinking. In the first he encouraged scholars to set aside what they had learned and to think for themselves. In the second he offered the same advice to preachers. In addition, he criticized every organized religion for creating unnecessary rules. Conservative scholars and ministers were so enraged by these ideas, and particularly by "The Divinity School Address," that Emerson was effectively banished from the Harvard campus for decades.

Despite such a hostile response from community leaders in Massachusetts, Emerson's beliefs soon attracted a wide audience. In particular, young writers and thinkers were drawn to his fresh ideas and his writing style, which was more colorful and poetic than most other philosophical styles. Under his guidance, they founded the Transcendental Club in 1836 as a forum for the new ideas. They also started a magazine, *The Dial,* in 1840 to publish the writings of Emerson and his circle of friends. And they initiated a set of experiments based on Emerson's teachings: Alcott opened a school for children in 1834, where he taught according to transcendental principles; George Ripley organized a transcendental commune, Brook Farm, in 1841; Thoreau attempted a self-reliant lifestyle in his cabin on Walden Pond from 1845 to 1847; and Walt Whitman, inspired by Emerson, created a new kind of poetry with his 1855 volume, *Leaves of Grass.*

Emerson encouraged Americans to live thoughtful, meaningful lives. To this end, he adopted a variety of social causes. He was an especially outspoken critic of slavery, though he refused to join any antislavery organization that might limit his independent thought. Still, he exercised his greatest influence, and enjoyed his greatest fame, as a writer and a lecturer. Essays such as "Self-Reliance" (1841), "Circles" (1841), and "Experience" (1844) introduced new philosophic and literary possibilities to a young, democratic nation. Books like *Representative Men* (1850) expressed an optimistic view of world history and of America's future. And the success of Emerson's own career—his migration from the church to the lecture hall—proved that the nation would reward original thought.

Emerson's health and memory started to deteriorate in the years following the Civil War. Still considered the preeminent intellectual in the United States, he published less and made fewer public appearances, until he died of pneumonia on April 27, 1882. Large crowds flooded Concord to attend his funeral and celebrate his life. The nation's moral and intellectual leader for almost fifty years, Emerson had given Americans a new way to think about themselves, their country, and their bright future.

Nathaniel Hawthorne

Novelist of New England Life and History
1804–1864

Obsessed with the crimes of the American past, as well as with his own family's past, Nathaniel Hawthorne explored the limits of national as well as personal guilt in stories and novels that are now recognized as American classics.

Born in Salem, Massachusetts, in 1804, Nathaniel Hathorne (he would later add a "w" to the family name) was a descendant of a long-established

Salem family that included John Hathorne, a judge in the famous witchcraft trials of the 1690s. Once a bustling seaport town, Salem was a declining village during Hawthorne's childhood, and Hawthorne's widowed mother was forced to take her son to Maine during his teen years. Nevertheless, the town and its history would dominate his imagination for the rest of his life.

> She bore on her breast, in the curiously embroidered letter, a specimen of her delicate and imaginative skill of which the dames of a court might gladly have availed themselves, to add the richer and more spiritual adornment of human ingenuity to their fabrics of silk and gold.
>
> ~ From *The Scarlet Letter*

Between 1821 and 1825, Hawthorne attended Bowdoin College in Maine. Among his classmates were Henry Wadsworth Longfellow, the future poet, and Franklin Pierce, the future U.S. president. Hawthorne did little to distinguish himself during his college years, however, and he returned with his mother to Salem immediately after graduation. For the next twelve years, he tried to build a career as a writer of magazine articles and short stories. Yet, though his work was occasionally published in the influential *Democratic Review,* he could not make a living solely with his pen. His first novel, an 1828 account of his Bowdoin years entitled *Fanshawe,* sold poorly, and Hawthorne burned the remaining copies. In 1837 he collected his best stories into the volume *Twice-Told Tales,* which received a favorable review from the influential critic and story writer Edgar Allan Poe but little other notice. Only his children's stories, collected in *Grandfather's Chair* (1841)—and in later volumes such as *Tanglewood Tales for*

Girls and Boys (1853)—captured the public's attention. But Hawthorne aspired to a different kind of literary fame.

In 1839, unable to survive by his writing alone, Hawthorne took a job at the Boston Custom House. Unfortunately, his duties took too much time away from his fiction. So in 1841 he joined some of his literary and artistic friends from Boston—most of whom were members of the transcendentalist movement surrounding the philosopher Ralph Waldo Emerson—to create a commune west of Boston called Brook Farm. Hawthorne hoped that life on the farm would allow him more time for his writing. But when he realized that the farm labor would also prove too restrictive, he left Brook Farm and settled in Concord, in the Old Manse, a home built by the Emerson family. Beginning a family of his own with his new wife, Sophia Peabody, and living at the center of the transcendentalist movement, he wrote and published some of his best short stories—including "Young Goodman Brown" and "Roger Malvin's Burial"—which were later collected in *Mosses From an Old Manse* (1846). Critics began to recognize his talent as a writer of dense, symbolic stories about sin and guilt, but *Mosses* failed to attract a broad readership, and once again Hawthorne was forced to search for more lucrative employment.

He worked in the Salem Custom House from 1846 to 1849, in a job he owed to his membership in the Democratic Party. He lost the job during a change in political leadership, but it had provided him with enough free time to draft the novel that would become his masterpiece: *The Scarlet Letter* (1850). Set in seventeenth-century Salem, *The Scarlet Letter* is the story of a Puritan woman, Hester Prynne, who is sentenced to wear an "A" on her clothes as punishment for adultery, a crime she committed while believing her husband had died. Her sense of guilt, along with the suffering of the minister who shared in her crime, occupies the center of the novel and becomes a means for

Hawthorne to explore New England's spiritual past as well as his family's Puritan history.

A year later, while living in Lenox, Massachusetts, near his friend and admirer Herman Melville, he continued his exploration of New England history by writing *The House of Seven Gables* (1851). The story of the Pyncheon family and their unusual house, both of which are haunted by the crimes of the past—in this case a murder and a corrupt land deal that results in the Pyncheons' rise to power—*The House of Seven Gables* combined Hawthorne's historical studies with his first analysis of life in his own era. It was followed by another story collection, *The Snow-Image and Other Twice Told Tales* (1852), and a novel based on his experiences at Brook Farm, *The Blithedale Romance* (1852).

A year after the publication of *The House of Seven Gables,* Hawthorne returned to Concord to write a biography of his college friend Franklin Pierce, who was then running for president. Pierce appreciated Hawthorne's efforts and, after he was elected in 1853, appointed Hawthorne his consul to the British city of Liverpool. The writer performed ambassadorial functions until Pierce lost the party nomination to be reelected in 1857. Hawthorne then moved to Italy and lived among American artists in Rome, collecting material for his final novel, *The Marble Faun* (1860), an account of the expatriate experience in Europe.

Hawthorne returned to the United States on the eve of the Civil War, but as his loyalty to the unpopular Pierce had proven, he was out of touch with the political atmosphere of the nation. Nevertheless, he was one of the United State's most famous and popular writers when he died in 1864, a year before the conclusion of the war.

Since the publication of *The Scarlet Letter,* Hawthorne has occupied a central place in American literary history. His best works, published at a time when

Americans were still seeking their own literature—one that addressed American themes and could be distinguished from the works of Europe—introduced a new subtlety and poetic quality into American writing. They quickly became the standard against which other American novels and short stories were judged. And for his insights into the American past, and especially the crimes that took place at the founding of the nation, Hawthorne continued to provide inspiration to American writers from Henry James to Robert Lowell, who were interested in a refined analysis of the national character.

Henry Wadsworth Longfellow

Popular Poet, Influential Scholar
1807–1882

To American audiences of the mid-nineteenth century, no writer was as recognizable or as important as Henry Wadsworth Longfellow. Although modern readers tend to favor more complicated, less sentimental poetry than the musical rhymes Longfellow produced, the simplicity and grace of his poems were precisely the characteristics that made him popular

> Thou, too, sail on, O Ship of State!
> Sail on, O Union, strong and great!
> Humanity with all its fears,
> With all the hopes of future years,
> Is hanging breathless on thy fate!
>
> ⁓ From "The Building of the Ship"

and revered in his time. And as a chief creator of fine literature in the young nation, Longfellow exerted a tremendous influence on American society, offering up many of the stories and myths that have come to define the national culture.

Longfellow was born on February 27, 1807, in Portland, Maine (a territory of Massachusetts until 1820). From an early age, he aspired to literary fame. He pursued this goal at Portland Academy and Bowdoin College in Brunswick, Maine, where he befriended the future novelist Nathaniel Hawthorne. After graduating in 1825, he spent four years in Europe, studying foreign languages. He returned to Bowdoin in 1829 as a foreign language professor. After six years at Bowdoin, he took another visit to Europe, during which his first wife died. Longfellow returned to the United States in 1836 and moved to Cambridge, Massachusetts, where he would live for the rest of his life. He accepted a professorship at Harvard University and wrote and published in a variety of genres including sketches, scholarly articles, textbooks, and, especially, poetry.

With the publication of his first book of poems, 1839's *Voices of the Night*, he earned a place at the center of American literary society, and his Cambridge home, Craigie House, became a gathering place for other young writers. Longfellow became the nation's leading literary authority as well as its most popular poet. For the next thirty years, he wrote short and long poems on a variety of topics. Most important, he introduced American themes into poetry.

Before Longfellow, much of American poetry had been concerned with European ideas and adapted from European models. But with the publication of works like the poem of colonial life *Evangeline* (1847), the Native American epic *The Song of Hiawatha* (1855), and *The Courtship of Miles Standish* (1858), based on the Pilgrims' experiences at Plymouth, Longfellow turned the nation's attention to its own history and culture. He also addressed American politics, and especially the debates that led up to the Civil War, in volumes such as *Poems on Slavery* (1842) and *The Seaside and the Fireside* (1850), which included the nationalist poem "The Building of the Ship."

After the death of his second wife in 1861, Longfellow changed direction and wrote increasingly spiritual poetry, including an English translation of Dante Alighieri's *Divine Comedy,* an epic poem about the afterlife. But he also continued to explore American themes in a series of plays and volumes including 1863's *Tales of a Wayside Inn,* which included the children's favorite "Paul Revere's Ride."

In his poems, plays, stories, and essays, Longfellow turned both his knowledge of history and his own personal tragedies into the basis of a new, patriotic American culture. For his purely American themes and his skillful meters and rhymes, he was revered in both the United States and England. By the time of his death in 1882, he had become the nation's leading literary ambassador and one of its few internationally acclaimed writers.

Edgar Allan Poe

Editor, Poet, Master of the Short Story
1809–1849

The son of poor stage actors, Edgar Allan Poe was orphaned before he was three years old. Although he was raised by John Allan, a wealthy merchant from Richmond, Virginia, Poe never quite fit in to his adoptive family. He was haunted by his mother's death, erratic in his behavior, and often spiteful. Allan, a serious and demanding figure, was often disappointed in young Edgar. Yet Poe was determined to succeed in American society. And he ultimately achieved the fame and influence he sought by turning his personal tragedies into ghostly, obsessive stories and poems, including some of the greatest master-pieces of American literature.

> True!—nervous—very, very dreadfully nervous I had been and am; but why *will* you say that I am mad? The disease had sharpened my senses—not destroyed—not dulled them.
>
> ⮜ From "The Tell-Tale Heart"

As a young man, Poe lived an aimless and unfocused life, drifting in and out of schools and jobs. For a short time, he attended the University of Virginia. Then he enlisted in the army. He even attended the U.S. Military Academy at West Point, New York. But he could not complete anything he started, often because of his own misbehavior. Only his poetry held his attention. He managed to publish three volumes, *Tamerlane and Other Poems* (1827), *Al Aaraaf* (1829), and *Poems* (1831), while the rest of his life appeared in disarray. Confident in his literary skill, Poe finally decided that he would make his name in America's growing literary industry. It was a daring choice: The public did not favorably receive his early poetry.

Poe's primary goal was to operate and write for a literary magazine of his own. But despite his literary talent, he had a reputation for being unpredictable and dishonest. Few investors trusted him to run a business without oversight. So instead of buying a magazine, he made his mark as an editor for popular journals such as *The Southern Literary Messenger, Graham's Magazine,* and *The Broadway Journal.* In these and other magazines, Poe published his fiery, entertaining brand of literary criticism. He became famous for his attacks against even the most celebrated writers in America. The most popular poet in the country, Henry Wadsworth Longfellow, was one of his favorite targets. Poe's harsh, sarcastic style did not make him very popular with other writers, but it sold magazines. And in his less vicious articles, Poe proved to be an intelligent and astute judge of literature. In this way, he managed to provide the country with new standards for good writing.

During his lifetime he was best known, and often despised, for his work as a critic. But his later reputation was based on his skill as a poet and as a writer of short stories. His most famous poem, "The Raven," created a popular sensation when it was published in 1845. A haunting meditation on death, it featured a rhythmic, musical style. He had been writing in this style for years, introducing it in early poems such as "The Sleeper," and he would continue to develop it in later poems including "Annabel Lee" and "The Bells." But "The Raven" was considered the high point of his poetic career.

Death and mourning, the subjects of his best poems, also became the themes of his greatest fiction. In tales such as "The Fall of the House of Usher" (1839), "The Pit and the Pendulum" (1842), "The Tell-Tale Heart" (1843), and "The Cask of Amontillado" (1846), Poe transformed the anger, loss, and sense of abandonment he experienced at a young age into some of the most chilling stories in American literature. These stories also exhibited the precise control Poe exercised over his best writing, as he presented unexpected, frightening plot twists in beautiful language. They made him the most important American writer in the style known as Gothic, which often featured haunted castles, ghosts, and other horror-story and science-fiction features.

But nowhere was Poe's literary control more evident than in his mysteries "The Murders in the Rue Morgue" (1841), "The Gold Bug" (1843), "The Mystery of Marie Rogêt" (1842–3), and "The Purloined Letter" (1844).

Considered the first detective stories ever written, these works combined Poe's interests in scientific investigation with his desire to shock his audience. They combined the plot twists of Gothic stories with exercises in logic and deduction to create a new literary genre.

The vast majority of Poe's articles, poems, and stories were published in magazines, a relatively new medium in the early nineteenth century. Poe, a true lover of the medium, tried to raise magazine writing to the level of high art. He often succeeded. Sadly, he was less successful in his personal life. Beginning with the death of his mother, he was continually tormented by tragedy. The worst blow was the death of his young wife, Virginia, in 1847. Broken by her death and defeated by his personal and literary foes, Poe struggled with his own sicknesses, including alcoholism, as well as his poverty until his final days. When he died on October 7, 1849, his reputation was in jeopardy. His writings were more popular in Europe than in the United States, where he had made many enemies with his harsh criticism and difficult personality. But since his death, Poe has been recognized and celebrated as one of the most important writers of the past two centuries: a journalism pioneer, a gifted Gothic writer, and the father of the modern detective story.

Harriet Beecher Stowe

Author of Antislavery Novel, Uncle Tom's Cabin
1811–1896

Born into a family of prominent clergymen and reformers, Harriet Beecher Stowe joined the most important reform movement in American history, the antislavery campaign of the 1840s and 1850s, and wrote its most famous and successful document, the novel *Uncle Tom's Cabin*. Though she wrote eleven other novels during her long life, as well as articles, poems, and stories, it was this first novel that helped change the course of American history and sealed her reputation as a major literary force.

Her father, Lyman Beecher, was a prominent Congregational minister and one of the leaders of the United States temperance movement, which sought to ban the consumption of alcoholic beverages. In his deeply religious, socially conscious household, he raised thirteen children, including seven future ministers. Harriet's brother Henry would become a pastor in Brooklyn and the country's most famous preacher; her sister Catharine would pioneer efforts in women's education. But Harriet did not initially pursue a life of public service. In 1836 she married Calvin Stowe, a teacher at her father's school in Cincinnati, the Lane Theological Seminary, and together they raised seven children. To earn extra money for her growing household, she taught in her sister's schools and published articles and stories, but she did not find her true literary voice until she became engaged in the Fugitive Slave Crisis.

When Congress passed the Fugitive Slave law in 1850, requiring all U.S. citizens (even those opposed to slavery) to aid in the capture of runaway slaves from the South, antislavery activists renewed their efforts to abolish slavery. Stowe, who had been writing abolitionist articles for Cincinnati newspapers,

> In that dizzy moment her feet to her scarce seemed to touch the ground, and a moment brought her to the water's edge. Right on behind her they came; and nerved with strength such as God gives only to the desperate, with one wild cry and flying leap, she vaulted sheer over the turbid current by the shore, on to the raft of ice beyond.
>
> ~ From *Uncle Tom's Cabin*

UNCLE TOM'S CABIN;

OR,

LIFE AMONG THE LOWLY.

BY

HARRIET BEECHER STOWE.

VOL. I.

BOSTON:
JOHN P. JEWETT & COMPANY.
CLEVELAND, OHIO:
JEWETT, PROCTOR & WORTHINGTON.
1852.

FIRST EDITION, IN THE EXCESSIVELY RARE
RED CLOTH PRESENTATION BINDING

When asked what inspired her to write *Uncle Tom's Cabin*, Harriet Beecher Stowe replied, "I wrote what I did because as a woman, as a mother, I was oppressed and broken-hearted with the sorrow and injustice I saw."

decided to write a book about the fugitives and their misfortunes. After researching slaves' lives in the South, she drafted *Uncle Tom's Cabin or, Life Among the Lowly*, which was published as a serial in *National Era* magazine in 1851 and 1852, and as a single volume in late 1852. Selling as many as 10,000 copies in a week and 300,000 copies in its first year, *Uncle Tom's Cabin* became an American publishing phenomenon.

By focusing on the positive relationships among individual slaves as well as the relationships, positive and negative, between slaves and their white masters, Stowe encouraged her audience to sympathize with slaves on a personal level. Although her novel was not entirely free of the racial prejudices of its era, it humanized the slaves in a way that was unusual in the 1850s. It reminded readers that slaves were mothers, fathers, and caring friends and that slavery disrupted the most sacred American institution: the family.

Later generations of Americans reinterpreted the novel's imagery and characters, often negatively. To civil rights activists of the twentieth century, peace-loving, humble characters such as Uncle Tom seemed distasteful, counterproductive, and even dangerous. And even in its time, the book had many detractors: Southern writers derided the novel as an exaggeration of plantation conditions; Northerners berated Stowe either for encouraging law-breaking behavior or for representing slaves as simple, harmless, and submissive. But in the years before the Civil War, *Uncle Tom's Cabin* was a radical antislavery statement. It changed the country's ideas about the Fugitive Slave Law, and about slavery in general. *Uncle Tom's Cabin* and its many imitators and stage adaptations involved new groups of people in the antislavery campaign, consolidating Northern opposition to Southern slavery as the conflict reached a boiling point.

After the astounding success of *Uncle Tom's Cabin,* Stowe turned her attention to other social causes and wrote novels at a rapid rate, often to alleviate her family's financial problems. But Stowe—who spent her later years in Hartford, Connecticut, in a house next to Mark Twain's residence—would never again find a subject as important as slavery, nor would she write a novel as popular, entertaining, and influential as *Uncle Tom's Cabin.* A milestone best-seller, it helped bring about the emancipation of the slaves, the most profound social change in U.S. history, and revealed the enormous power of popular culture in America. And it continues to serve as a model for politically engaged, activist literature in American society.

Frederick Douglass

Escaped Slave, Leading Abolitionist
1817(?)–1895

The struggle to abolish slavery depended on the cooperation of thousands. Politicians and clergymen, men and women, whites and blacks all worked together in the cause of freedom. By the beginning of the Civil War in 1861, entire armies were dedicating their lives to the cause. But among these champions of liberty, Frederick Douglass, who escaped slavery to become one of the nation's most eloquent writers, editors, and speakers, was perhaps the most influential. The most important African American writer and political figure of the nineteenth century, he proved the equality of the races at a time when even anti-slavery activists treated African Americans as inferiors.

Born Frederick Augustus Bailey, Douglass never knew his father; barely knew his mother, a slave from Talbot County, Maryland; and never knew his own birthday. Initially raised by relatives on a plantation, he was

> It was a glorious resurrection, from the tomb of slavery, to the heaven of freedom. My long-crushed spirit rose, cowardice departed, bold defiance took its place; and I now resolved that, however long I might remain a slave in form, the day had passed forever when I could be a slave in fact.
>
> ~ From *Narrative of the Life of Frederick Douglass, an American Slave*

sent to Baltimore before he was nine years old to serve the family of his master. As a slave growing up in a big city, Douglass enjoyed an unusual amount of freedom. He did not participate in the backbreaking labor that characterized plantation life, he was not confined to the poverty of plantation slave quarters, he was seldom whipped, and most remarkably, he learned to read and write. As a teenager, against his master's orders, Douglass educated himself by reading books and newspapers he found in the course of his workday. Armed with the knowledge he gathered from books, he dreamed of an escape to the free North.

In 1838, while working in a Baltimore shipyard, Douglass obtained fake documents claiming that he was a free man and used them to escape to New England. A fugitive slave in an unfamiliar region, he lived in constant fear of being captured and sent back to his masters. He assumed the name Frederick

Johnson, and later Frederick Douglass, to confuse slave catchers.

Settling in New Bedford, Massachusetts, Douglass continued to confront racial prejudice; no one would hire him to work as a caulker in the local shipyard. He therefore worked as an unskilled laborer until he could find some other means of supporting himself and his growing family. (Douglass and his wife would ultimately raise five children.) His break came in 1841, when he was asked to speak at an antislavery meeting in Nantucket, Massachusetts. Douglass astounded his white audience with his passion and eloquence. The American Anti-Slavery Society immediately hired him to travel the country as its spokesman. As a public speaker, he faced two dilemmas. First, he put himself in plain view of the slave catchers who were still trying to bring him back to Baltimore. Second, he had difficulty earning credibility; unable to believe that a slave could speak so brilliantly and intelligently, white audiences often doubted the truth of his story. In response to the first dilemma, Douglass kept moving for three years and occasionally fled to Europe to avoid capture. In response to the second dilemma, he wrote *Narrative of the Life of Frederick Douglass, an American Slave* in 1845 to prove that he had indeed been a slave.

Unusual among slave narratives of the era, Douglass's *Narrative* includes the actual names of owners and plantations. In this way, it ensures skeptical readers that it is a true account of a slave's life. The Douglass who emerges from *Narrative* is a resourceful, self-educated man who refuses to submit to his masters. Strong in body, mind, and spirit, he serves as a model of determination and persistence. In later autobiographies, including *My Bondage and My Freedom* (1855) and *Life and Times of Frederick Douglass* (1881), Douglass would expand his account and shift its emphasis to meet the changing political needs of the African American community. But the short, powerful *Narrative* of 1845, with its emphasis on personal strength and resistance, remains the classic account of slavery in American literature.

In 1847, Douglass's European friends purchased his freedom, allowing him to return to the United States without fear of capture. He settled in Rochester, New York, and founded *The North Star,* an antislavery newspaper. In *The North Star* as well as in his later journals, *Frederick Douglass's Weekly* and *Douglass's Monthly,* he began to criticize the pacifist abolitionist movement and, as he had in *Narrative,* call for a more active and occasionally violent resistance to slavery. For a short time, he supported radicals such as John Brown, who led bloody antislavery attacks in Kansas and at Harper's Ferry, Virginia, in the 1850s. Douglass also supported slavery's political opponents, such as the Liberty Party and the newly formed Republican Party. And he offered his house as a stop on the Underground Railroad, a secret network of people who helped slaves escape to the North and to Canada. By the beginning of the Civil War, he had earned the confidence of President Lincoln and helped recruit soldiers—including two of his sons—to fight in the Union's first black regiments.

After the war, Douglass returned to the podium to rally support for the Thirteenth Amendment, which abolished slavery; the Fourteenth Amendment, which expanded citizenship privileges to include any person born in the United States; and the Fifteenth Amendment, which granted all men the right to vote. He also championed women's equality and was the vice-presidential candidate of the Equal Rights Party in 1872. In his later years, he even held several government positions, including an ambassadorship to the Republic of Haiti.

Thus Douglass remained a powerful figure in the nation for more than fifty years, assembling a record of service that would have been remarkable in any context but was particularly remarkable for a man born into slavery. And through his writings, especially his 1845 *Narrative,* he remains a central figure in American culture today.

Henry David Thoreau

Transcendental Essayist, Nature Writer
1817–1862

In 1845, while living in a cabin beside Walden Pond in Concord, Massachusetts, Henry David Thoreau was arrested by local authorities. His crime: He refused to pay a tax levied on voters. It was the act of a radical thinker and a man willing to be imprisoned for his beliefs. Because the U.S. government supported slavery, Thoreau reasoned, all the tax money that the government collected supported slavery as well. And he preferred spending a night in jail to contributing even a single dollar to the slave system he hated.

Four years later, in 1849, he published a pamphlet based on his experience in jail. *Resistance to Civil Government,* also known as *Civil Disobedience,* encouraged nonviolent resistance to unjust laws. It eloquently expressed

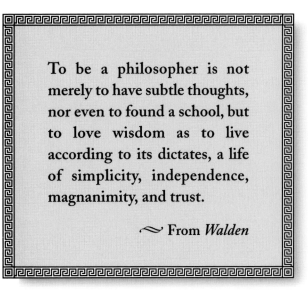

To be a philosopher is not merely to have subtle thoughts, nor even to found a school, but to love wisdom as to live according to its dictates, a life of simplicity, independence, magnanimity, and trust.

～ From *Walden*

Thoreau's desire to live a principled, moral life and influenced such twentieth-century champions of freedom as Mahatma Gandhi and Martin Luther King Jr. But in his own lifetime, Thoreau was an obscure figure, better known as a friend to famous and influential writers than as a writer himself.

Born in Concord on June 12, 1817, Thoreau was a gifted student who excelled in the local schools and attended Harvard University. Despite his contrary personality and stubborn nature, he graduated with honors and returned to Concord to open a successful school of his own. In Concord he befriended one of the most important figures in American literary history: Ralph Waldo Emerson. A poet, philosopher, essayist, and lecturer, Emerson led a group of northeastern intellectuals known as the transcendentalists. The transcendentalists' emphasis on intellectual and personal freedom, their desire for justice, their respect for nature, and their faith in the power of literature appealed to the young Thoreau, who soon moved into Emerson's house, where he worked as a caretaker.

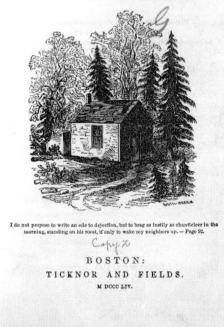

WALDEN;

OR,

LIFE IN THE WOODS.

BY HENRY D. THOREAU,

AUTHOR OF "A WEEK ON THE CONCORD AND MERRIMACK RIVERS."

I do not propose to write an ode to dejection, but to brag as lustily as chanticleer in the morning, standing on his roost, if only to wake my neighbors up. — Page 92.

Copy 2

BOSTON:

TICKNOR AND FIELDS.

M DCCC LIV.

Since its publication in 1854, Thoreau's *Walden* has been reprinted in over 200 editions, and in over forty foreign languages.

Thoreau was unusual among the transcendentalists in that he honestly tried to live the self-sufficient lifestyle that Emerson described in his writings. In 1845 he built a cabin by Walden Pond, on land owned by Emerson, and began his now-famous experiment in living simply and independently. He grew his own vegetables, made many of the tools he needed, and gave up luxuries. While at Walden, he completed his account of a journey he had taken with his brother John, *A Week on the Concord and Merrimack Rivers* (1849), laid the groundwork for *Civil Disobedience*, and kept the detailed journals he would later edit and release as *Walden, or Life in the Woods* (1854).

Part memoir, part philosophical treatise, part natural history, *Walden* chronicles Thoreau's two-year project of self-discovery and is now widely considered one of the most distinctive works in American literature. In it, Thoreau perfected a writing style that is both scholarly and conversational, mixing everyday observations with deep insights into literature, religion, and nature. And he provided Americans with a model for living simply.

Returning to Concord after abandoning the Walden project, Thoreau continued to write. He published sparingly, however, to little popular notice, and had to take a variety of jobs, including one in his father's pencil factory, to support himself. Still, he did manage to participate in the popular lecture circuit of the era, arguing in favor of the abolition of slavery in addresses such as "Slavery in Massachusetts" (1854). He even assisted some slaves who escaped to freedom along the secret network known as the Underground Railroad. But he neither sought nor achieved fame during his short life.

In late 1860, after a walk through the countryside on a cold winter day, Thoreau began to suffer from tuberculosis, the same disease that had killed his father. He died in Concord on May 6, 1862, as he was compiling his best essays for publication. Posthumously published in volumes including *Excursions* (1863), those essays as well as *Walden* and *Civil Disobedience* would reach a wider audience than their author had ever imagined. And Thoreau himself would become a hero to generations of Americans who wished to follow their consciences during difficult times.

Herman Melville

Writer of Complex Novels, Including Moby-Dick
1819–1891

One of America's most challenging fiction writers, Herman Melville was considered a literary failure at the time of his death in 1891. Having rejected the formula of his successful seafaring novels of the 1840s, he attempted to combine popular fiction and intense philosophical inquiry in a series of experimental works in the 1850s, including *Moby-Dick,* only to lose his audience. But while readers rejected these novels during his lifetime, readers of the twentieth century rediscovered Melville's work and promoted him to the ranks of the finest writers in the nation's history.

Melville was a descendent of wealthy and influential New York families. But by the time he was born in 1819, his own family's fortunes had begun to decline, culminating in his father's bankruptcy and early

> Call me Ishmael. Some years ago—never mind how long precisely—having little or no money in my purse, and nothing particular to interest me on shore, I thought I would sail about a little and see the watery part of the world.
>
> ～ From *Moby-Dick*

death when Melville was just twelve years old. Forced to contend with her reduced circumstances, Melville's mother moved her family to Albany, New York, where Herman attended school for a short time. He then held a variety of jobs such as teaching, clerking, and farming. He even sailed on a vessel bound for England, before he set out in 1841 for a long adventure as a cabin boy on *Acushnet*, a whaling ship. *Acushnet* followed whale migrations to the South Pacific where, eighteen months after he boarded, Melville deserted the ship to live among the inhabitants of the Marquesas Islands. A month later he boarded an Austrialian vessel, which he deserted in Tahiti, where he was imprisoned. Finally, after a stint on another whaling vessel and a brief visit to the Hawaiian Islands, he boarded a U.S. Navy ship and served until his discharge in 1844.

Having experienced more adventure in three years than most men experience in a lifetime, Melville returned to the United States to write about what he had

In the struggle between Moby-Dick and the crew of the *Pequod*, Melville created his most lasting imagery.

seen and done. His first book, an adventure story of the South Pacific entitled *Typee* (1846), was a popular success, as was its sequel, *Omoo* (1847). Later in 1847, Melville married Elizabeth Shaw, the daughter of the chief justice of the Massachusetts Supreme Court. He and his wife moved to Arrowhead, a farm in the Berkshire Mountains, near the home of friend and literary idol Nathaniel Hawthorne. Comfortable, settled, and inspired by Hawthorne, he seemed headed for a brilliant, successful literary career.

Yet Melville was uncomfortable with the attention he received—particularly with his readers' insistence that his novels be read as his own life story. He wished to write books that were less concerned with entertainment and more engaged in political and philosophical debate. In his next three sea novels—*Mardi* (1849), *Redburn* (1849), and *White-Jacket* (1850)—Melville transformed his experiences into broader symbols of human experience. Each book seemed more philosophically complex, more distant from the popular themes of his early successes, and less comprehensible to reading audiences, and his reputation began to suffer.

In 1850 he published the culmination of his literary and philosophical inquiries: *Moby-Dick; or, The Whale*. The story of Ahab, the captain of a whaling vessel (*The Pequod*) who endangers himself and his crew in his pursuit of the white whale that bit off a part of his leg, *Moby-Dick* is an unconventional novel in both its themes and its presentation. Although the story is narrated by Ishmael, one of the members of *The Pequod*'s crew, Melville frequently interrupts the narration with supplemental material—chapters about religion, sailing, the anatomy of whales, and a host of other topics—that complicate the novel without commenting directly on the plot. In this way he expands the novel's meanings and heightens its religious and political symbolism.

Contemporary audiences rejected the novel for its extraordinary length and complexity. Melville responded to their criticisms with *Pierre; or, The Ambiguities,* a novel that mocked the styles of fiction that were popular in the 1840s and 1850s while presenting a decidedly pessimistic view of human nature. Not surprisingly, *Pierre* was also a financial and critical failure and effectively ended Melville's career as a fiction writer. His 1856 short-story collection, *The Piazza Tales,* contained several masterpieces of the genre, including "Bartleby, the Scrivener" and "Benito Cereno," a brilliant portrayal of racial conflict and misunderstanding, but it did not resurrect his career. Nor did his 1855 novel about the Revolutionary War, *Israel Potter,* nor *The Confidence Man* (1857), a cynical satire of American culture set on a Mississippi riverboat.

A volume of his poetry about the Civil War, *Battle-Pieces and Aspects of the War* (1866), earned belated praise, but by the end of the war Melville had been forced to seek employment outside his literary endeavors. Discouraged and besieged by financial and family problems, he became a customs inspector in Manhattan. He published only three more volumes of poetry, including *Clarel* (1876), a book-length account of his 1857 pilgrimage to Jerusalem. During the last three years of life, however, Melville worked on a novella about his seafaring experiences. A symbolic account of a naive sailor's mutiny and the deliberations of the ship captain who must punish him, *Billy Budd, Sailor* is now considered a classic of American literature. But Melville was still working on it at the time of his death in 1891, and it was not published until 1924. Thus Melville died in obscurity, a forgotten writer whose greatest achievements had either been ignored for fifty years or not yet been published.

During the past century, Melville's status has improved dramatically. Scholars, critics, and general readers all recognize him as one of the nation's supreme fiction writers. Praised for the sweeping range of his imagination, for the power of his greatest works—*Moby-Dick,* "Benito Cereno," *Billy Budd*—and for the depth of his inquiries into American society and human nature, he has also earned a reputation for being one of the most modern thinkers among the nineteenth century's literary giants. In fact, the very qualities that made him an unpopular writer in the 1850s now secure him a place at the pinnacle of American literary history.

Susan Warner

Best-Selling Writer of Sentimental Fiction
1819–1885

Susan Warner's early life was comfortable and carefree. Her father, a successful New York lawyer, was able to provide her and her younger sister, Anna, with fine educations and time for leisure activities. According to some accounts, Susan developed into a bookish and rather spoiled young girl. But the good times did not last, and Susan was forced to change her lifestyle in order to survive. The most important product of that change, her novel *The Wide, Wide World,*

would make her famous and dominate the American publishing industry for more than fifty years.

When Warner was nine, her mother died, leaving the family in the care of a devoted aunt. When she was nineteen, her father lost most of his wealth in the financial panic of 1837, a banking crisis that wiped out entire fortunes and nearly crippled the American economy. Care of the family fell squarely onto her shoulders. Susan could no longer afford to enjoy the books and quiet entertainments that had dominated her childhood.

> Ellen had plenty of faults, but amidst them all love to her mother was the strongest feeling her heart knew. It had power enough now to move her as nothing else could have done.
>
> ∽ From *The Wide, Wide World*

Sad and depressed, she turned to religion for comfort. In 1844 she joined the Presbyterian church on Constitution Island, in the community beside the Hudson River that had become the family's permanent residence. The church gave new structure to her life, and she turned her back on many of her old comforts for good. She and her sister found purpose and fulfillment as charity workers and missionaries in New York City, spreading the warmth of their new faith. But these changes did not improve their financial situation. By 1848 their father was bankrupt, and Susan and Anna became responsible for the family's economic well-being. Anna created and marketed a children's game to keep them afloat as Susan began writing a novel, *The Wide, Wide World*, which was published in 1850.

Warner's own life provided the basic structure of her first novel. Like Warner, the novel's heroine, Ellen Montgomery, was raised in an affluent home. But, in the first few chapters of the book, Ellen experiences a series of hardships: her mother dies, her father loses his fortune, and she moves from a comfortable urban home to her aunt's country farm. The rest of the novel follows Ellen's spiritual education, as her guardians teach her lessons in self-denial and generosity and encourage her to retain her childlike innocence. Like most other sentimental novels of the nineteenth century—novels that explore feminine ideals and provide readers with models of moral purity—*The Wide, Wide World* challenges its heroine and forces her to grow spiritually, until she is deemed ready for marriage and finds a worthy husband, an important goal for a nineteenth-century woman.

The spiritual themes and raw emotions of the novel made it an instant hit; it was among the best-sellers of the nineteenth century in both America and England. But despite its enormous popularity, neither *The Wide, Wide World* nor Warner's second hit novel, *Queechy,* earned her enough money to support herself or her family. The pre–Civil War publishing industry was not structured to reward female writers, no matter how popular they were. So Susan and Anna earned money in a variety of ways: They co-wrote books about Christianity and morality, they took jobs grading papers for local schools, and they provided Bible classes to local students. Susan also continued to write novels.

Together, Susan and Anna managed to enjoy fulfilling lives despite their many hardships. But none of their achievements would ever top the success of *The Wide, Wide World.* By the time Susan Warner died in 1885, it was standard reading for Americans of both sexes and all ages.

Walt Whitman

Poet of American Democracy
1819–1892

Walt Whitman was the most idealistic writer in American history. An observer of the political struggles that gave rise to the Civil War, a participant in the war itself, and a proponent of national unity after the war, Whitman dedicated himself and his writing to the idea that the United States was one nation, indivisible. As a journalist and, more important, as a poet, he hoped that his writing would become the glue that held the nation together.

> I celebrate myself,
> And what I assume you shall assume,
> For every atom belonging to me as good belongs to you.
>
> I loafe and invite my soul,
> I lean and loafe at my ease. . .observing a spear of summer grass.
>
> ～ From *Leaves of Grass*

Whitman was born on Long Island, New York in 1819, the second son of Quaker parents, but grew up in Brooklyn. When his parents returned to Long Island in the 1830s, Whitman stayed behind to work as a newspaper printer in Brooklyn and nearby Manhattan. In 1836 he too returned to Long Island as a schoolteacher; he later became the editor of his own newspaper. But for a young man with serious literary aspirations, the towns of Long Island were too small. Whitman would always require the bustle and diversity of the big city for his best work.

In 1841 he began his career as a writer and reporter for Brooklyn and Manhattan newspapers. In the early nineteenth century, political parties operated most of the newspapers; because Whitman was a Democrat, most of his articles appeared in that party's journals. At the same time, he wrote his only novel, *Franklin Evans* (1842), as a contribution to the American temperance movement, which fought to limit the consumption of alcohol. (Whitman's father and two of his brothers may have struggled with alcoholism.) But by the late 1840s, Whitman, like the rest of the country, became obsessed with a different political issue: slavery.

In 1848 he founded *The Brooklyn Freeman,* a newspaper calling for the federal government to halt the expansion of slavery in the Western territories. This paper ended his association with the Democratic Party, which tended to support slavery. During this period he also began writing poetry. By leaving the Democratic Party and experimenting with new kinds of writing, Whitman prepared himself for the most important work of his life.

Whitman's best poems are written in a style known as free verse, featuring long, rhythmic lines but no clear rhyme scheme. They also feature long, descriptive lists of people, places, and objects. Few American readers had ever seen such poetry when Whitman's first verses appeared in the early 1850s. Fewer understood the unusual goal Whitman had set for his work. With free verse, Whitman wished to offer something new and liberating, poetry worthy of a young democracy like the United States. And in his lists, he tried to represent every possible view of American culture, from the life of a president to the life of a servant. As disagreements over slavery occupied more and more of the nation's attention and civil war seemed inevitable, Whitman hoped that his poetry would provide people with images of a healthy, unified America. He hoped to prevent a violent crisis.

In 1855 he collected his poems and published them under the title *Leaves of Grass*. The volume received little notice, but Ralph Waldo Emerson, the most influential intellectual in the country (and one of the writers who had inspired Whitman to experiment with poetry in the first place), praised his work and encouraged him to continue. Soon Whitman attracted a small audience of devoted followers.

But the slavery debate finally split the country in 1861, and the Civil War temporarily interrupted Whitman's writing career. Disappointed that his poetry had little effect on the divided nation, Whitman volunteered to work as a nurse for the Union army in late 1862. Living in Washington, D.C., he held several low-level government appointments and spent most of his time in hospitals, visiting sick and dying soldiers. From these experiences, he would write the war poems of *Drum-Taps* (1865)—which, like all of his other poems, would be absorbed into later editions of *Leaves of Grass* (Whitman prepared nine editions of the collection). Whitman would also write his two most famous poems, "O Captain! My Captain!" and "When Lilacs Last in the Dooryard Bloom'd," following the 1865 assassination of his hero, Abraham Lincoln.

Whitman remained in Washington after the war, holding government jobs while continuing to write. He also became the subject of intense debate, as many readers and critics began objecting to the graphic depictions of the human body in his poetry. Rather than ruining his career, however, the controversy increased his fame. By 1873, when he moved to Camden, New Jersey, to live with his brother George, Whitman was able to find work as a lecturer. He was also able to find publishers for new editions of *Leaves of Grass* as well as memoirs including *Specimen Days* (1882) and *November Boughs* (1888). Though he was unable to save money from these ventures and became dependent upon the generosity of his fans in his later years, he finally received the praise and attention he had sought throughout his career. Collections of his poetry were published in Europe, and visiting foreign dignitaries and writers, such as Irish playwright Oscar Wilde, would stop in Camden to see the man known as "the good, gray poet."

Whitman had suffered the first of a series of strokes during his Civil War service, and poor health plagued him for the rest of his life. But before he died in 1892, Whitman saw his influence spread from a handful of northeastern readers to an international following, a following that has only grown since his death. He may not have achieved his initial goal of preventing the Civil War, but he did revolutionize the way poets write. He also provided the United States with some its most distinctive poetry.

Emily Dickinson

Poet of Personal Spirituality
1830–1886

Emily Dickinson avoided public life so completely, and left so little record of her daily activities and concerns, that she remains a mystery to later generations of American readers. What is certain is that she composed an extraordinary number of beautiful and challenging poems (almost 2,000) that now occupy a central position in American literature. Dickinson was born in 1830 in Amherst, Massachusetts, a town her family had helped to found. The

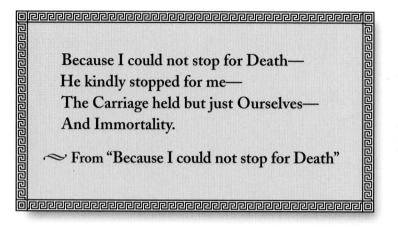

Because I could not stop for Death—
He kindly stopped for me—
The Carriage held but just Ourselves—
And Immortality.

~ From "Because I could not stop for Death"

Dickinsons remained prominent in western Massachusetts throughout Emily's life. Her father was a lawyer and an officer of nearby Amherst College, and he was elected to the U.S. House of Representatives in 1852; her brother Austin shared in the family law practice. The Dickinson home was therefore a busy place, visited frequently by important figures from the local political and educational circles. Emily, who was once thought to have lived a lonely life, actually grew up at the busy center of Amherst society.

An intelligent and willful girl, she received the standard education for a woman of her era and social position. In her early teens, she attended Amherst Academy. Then, during the 1847–48 school year, she studied at nearby Mount Holyoke Female Seminary (now known as Mount Holyoke College). During this period, she began displaying her literary talents. Her letters to friends and family members ripple with keen observations, wit, and a rare eloquence. Unfortunately, she fell ill during her first year at Mount Holyoke, and her father decided not to send her back for another term. For the rest of her life, she would pursue her education through the local library and her father's collection of books.

Between 1848 and 1855, Dickinson frequently traveled through Massachusetts, from Boston to Springfield, visiting friends. She also stayed with her father in Washington, D.C., during his congressional term. But after 1855 she left the Amherst area only twice, both times to receive treatment in

Boston for eye ailments. Instead, she stayed close to home, caring for her sickly mother and, especially after 1858, writing poetry.

Dickinson's poems remain among the most distinct in American literature. She was never a member of an organized church, but her best poems explore her spiritual concerns: questions about universal order; God's influence in ordinary life; death and the afterlife. These were common themes in nineteenth-century American literature, but no one had ever approached them the way Dickinson did. Her poems feature short, rhymed lines that seem simple at first glance. Often they sound like standard melodic verse. But her word choices are complicated, her imagery is abstract, and her poems demand an intense concentration from readers. Later generations of poets would follow her example to create poetry that would be both challenging and beautiful.

For her personal enjoyment, Dickinson collected groups of her poems and bound them into handmade books. But she officially published only a handful of poems during her lifetime and rarely sought a wider audience. In 1862 she sent some of her work to an influential Boston editor, Thomas Wentworth Higginson. But Higginson misunderstood her innovative approach to poetry and discouraged her from publishing more. (In 1890, four years after Dickinson's death, Higginson would finally edit and publish the first collection of her work.)

The vast majority of her poems therefore remained hidden from the public during her lifetime. She would read them to friends, include them in letters, or hide them away in her bedroom. But she would not seek fame through them. Nor would she use them to extend her influence beyond Amherst. During the last thirty years of her life, she appears to have been satisfied with a few close friendships, an extensive correspondence, and of course, her poetry. She died in 1886, without receiving the recognition she deserved for producing one of the most remarkable bodies of work in American literature.

Louisa May Alcott

Children's Author, Social Reformer
1832–1888

ouisa May Alcott was one of the greatest writers of children's literature in American history. Her chronicles of the fictional March family—*Little Women* (1868–69), *Little Men* (1871), and *Jo's Boys* (1886)—remain among the classics of the genre and have been popular favorites since they first appeared. Not surprisingly, it was Alcott's own childhood that provided the material for her best work and set her apart from other writers of her era.

Born in Germantown, Pennsylvania, in 1832, Louisa May was the second of four daughters of Bronson Alcott, a pioneering educator, a philosopher, and after moving the family to Boston, a prominent member of the transcendentalist circle of the 1830s and 1840s. Writers and philosophers such as Ralph

> Yet it was a hard time for sensitive, high-spirited Jo, who meant so well and had apparently done so ill. But it did her good, for those whose opinion had real value gave her the criticism which is an author's best education, and when the first soreness was over, she could laugh at her poor little book, yet believe in it still.
>
> ~ From *Little Women*

Waldo Emerson and Henry David Thoreau counted Bronson Alcott among their closest friends and assisted in educating his daughters. Thus Louisa May received her instruction from some of the finest and most influential thinkers in American history. Yet her father proved too eccentric and distracted by intellectual matters to provide for his family. As a result, Louisa May was determined at a very early age to put her intellectual gifts to practical use. Although she would always remember her childhood fondly, she decided never to repeat her father's mistakes.

To help support her family, she worked at a variety of jobs during her teen years. But she soon realized that she would achieve true economic stability only with her pen. Writing under an assumed name, she published a series of melodramatic short stories that attracted a wide audience. Her first book, a collection of fairy tales entitled *Flower Fables,* was published in 1854 and seemed to solidify her reputation as a writer of fantasies. But the Civil War interrupted her writing career and changed the American audience's expectations for literature.

Drawn to the most important historical event of her era and determined to assist the soldiers, Alcott traveled to Washington, D.C., in 1862 to serve as a nurse in the city's hospitals. She treated the sick and wounded for less than a month before she contracted typhoid fever. Her letters home, in which she described her surroundings, became the substance of her second book, *Hospital Sketches* (1863). And the war itself would serve as a backdrop for some of the enormously successful fiction she would write in the following decades.

After the moderate success of her first novel, *Moods* (1864), Alcott accepted an editorial position with *Merry's Museum*, a magazine that printed children's literature. Her publisher then suggested that she attempt to write her own story for children. The result was *Little Women*, an episodic novel chronicling the adventures of the March sisters: Meg, Jo, Beth, and Amy. A semiautobiographical account of Alcott's own childhood in New England, *Little Women* was an instant success, prompting its publishers to request a second part, published to great fanfare in 1869. Though designed to provide its young readers with moral lessons, the novel was among the first to attempt realistic character development in American children's literature. The character of Jo, who was modeled on Alcott herself, proved rich enough to support two sequels, *Little Men, Life at Plumfield with Jo's Boys,* and *Jo's Boys and How They Turn Out.* In between the stories of the March family, Alcott published a variety of other novels for children, all of which proved immensely popular and made her a literary celebrity.

As the nation's best writer of juvenile fiction, Alcott achieved the financial security she sought. In her later years, this security freed her to participate in several of the era's reform movements, including the women's suffrage movement of the 1870s. Her commitment to social issues, as well as her commitment to the education of children, suggested that she had learned several important lessons from her eccentric father. She combined his idealism with her own professionalism to achieve lasting fame and influence. So when father and daughter died, two days apart in 1888, they left behind an important family legacy of intellectual and moral instruction. In addition, Louisa May Alcott left behind one of the most entertaining bodies of work in American literature.

Horatio Alger

Novelist Best Known for Rags-to-Riches Stories
1832–1899

Stories about poor boys who, through honest dealings and hard work, rise to the top of American society were not new when Horatio Alger published *Ragged Dick* in 1867. Founding fathers such as Benjamin Franklin, in *Poor Richard's Almanack* and in his autobiography, had experimented with the "rags to riches" story. But Alger wrote some of the most memorable stories in this genre, including the best-seller *Ragged Dick,* and produced them at a time when Americans needed them most. As a result, American "rags to riches" stories have been known as "Horatio Alger stories" ever since.

Alger was not a child of poverty like his later fictional characters. Born in 1832 in Revere, Massachusetts, he was the son of a prominent Unitarian minister. Intelligent and determined to pursue a career as a writer, he attended

> It was indeed a bright prospect for a boy who, only a year before, could neither read nor write, and depended for a night's lodging upon the chance hospitality of an alley-way or old wagon. Dick's great ambition to 'grow up 'spectable' seemed likely to be accomplished after all.
>
> ~ From *Ragged Dick*

Harvard College, where he excelled at most literary endeavors and earned high honors. In the years immediately following his graduation in 1852, he published stories, articles, and poems in literary magazines and journals throughout the country. But writers were poorly paid in the mid-nineteenth century, and Alger was soon forced to search for a new occupation.

Following in his father's footsteps, he returned to Harvard to study religion and was ordained a Unitarian minister in 1864. His first ministerial experience, serving a congregation in Brewster, Massachusetts, was not a happy one, however. He was unsuited to a life in the clergy, and a series of local scandals tarnished his reputation and cost him his job. In 1866, after promising to quit the ministry for good, he fled his church and moved to New York City. There he tried once again to make his way as a writer.

Given the misfortune that had befallen him in the mid-1860s, the success of his first children's novel, *Ragged Dick or, Street Life in New York with the*

Boot Blacks (1867), was itself a kind of "rags to riches" story. In this tale about a poor shoe-shine boy whose wisdom, honesty, and willingness to work hard result in his ultimate success as a businessman, Alger captured both the nation's faith in industry after the Civil War and its longstanding belief in individual achievement. The novel suggested that by upholding certain values and by avoiding certain temptations, even the poorest orphan could leave the city streets and create a comfortable, fulfilling life for himself. In real life, of course, such a transition was more difficult to achieve; poverty was not so easily defeated in an age of expanding cities and factory labor. But Alger's novel appealed to a wide variety of Americans precisely because of its optimistic and reassuring message; *Ragged Dick* restored people's faith in the American Dream. It soon became a best-seller, and Alger, after years of searching, finally found his place in American literature.

Following this initial success, Alger produced similar stories at a rapid rate. By the time he died, in 1899, he had written more than one hundred additional stories for boys, all of which were variations on the themes he first explored in *Ragged Dick:* hard work, honesty, persistence. Among the most popular were 1869's *Luck and Pluck* and 1871's *Tattered Tom.* So even though *Ragged Dick* was his only best-seller, Alger enjoyed a prosperous career. He never became the great novelist he had aspired to be, but through his writing he managed to overcome personal hardship as well as provide generations of Americans with stories of hope—stories that celebrated the opportunity at the core of American society.

Mark Twain

Humorist, Satirist, and Celebrated Novelist
1835–1910

*S*amuel Langhorne Clemens grew up in Hannibal, Missouri, a small town on the banks of the Mississippi River. In that town, Clemens trained to become a printer, worked as a reporter, and most significantly, learned to navigate the Mississippi itself. As a young man, Clemens became a riverboat pilot, a job that enabled him to collect many of the stories he would later adapt into his popular novels and lectures. The job also provided him with the pen

> But I reckon I got to light out for the Territory ahead of the rest, because Aunt Sally she's going to adopt me and sivilize me and I can't stand it. I been there before.
>
> ~ From *Adventures of Huckleberry Finn*

name he would make famous: Mark Twain.

"Mark twain" was what the riverboat pilots would shout to indicate that the river was two fathoms (about 12 feet) deep, deep enough to allow a riverboat to pass safely. As riverboat traffic decreased in the late 1800s, with the faster and more powerful railroads replacing the boats, the phrase should have passed out of the language. But it remains in American culture to designate one of the nation's most beloved writers.

Because the residents of Hannibal held slaves, the townsmen fought for the Confederacy during the Civil War. When the war began in 1861, Clemens volunteered to fight as well. But he detested military discipline and deserted the army, heading west in pursuit of fame. Like many of the characters he would later create, Clemens was a lifelong schemer and a dreamer. Throughout his life, he entered into a variety of business ventures, including the mining business, in the hope of earning his fortune; almost all of them failed. During his time in California after the war, he achieved some renown—as Mark Twain—but only while working as a newspaper reporter and occasional lecturer in San Francisco. His dry sense of humor earned him the approval of the reading public, and his slow, ironic delivery made him a highly regarded stage performer. His ability with words earned for him what his business sense could not.

He finally realized his dreams in 1865, when he published the short story "The Celebrated Jumping Frog of Calaveras County." Based on a tale he had heard while in the Nevada gold mines, it became one of the most popular humorous sketches in the country. That one story extended his reputation to the East Coast as well as to Europe. Suddenly the man from Hannibal was an international celebrity. Following that initial success, Twain traveled the world and wrote about his experiences in a new, wry American voice.

Skeptical of authority and of anyone claiming superiority, the humorous voice of Mark Twain appealed to the readers of a youthful, democratic society. His first book-length work, 1869's *The Innocents Abroad,* chronicled his journey to foreign lands, comparing the United States favorably with every other nation he visited. In *Roughing It* (1872), he described his life in the western territories among the rascals and gamblers of frontier life. And in *The Gilded Age* (1873), in collaboration with his friend Charles Dudley Warner, he criticized the waste and greed that he observed at the top of American society after the Civil War. Though not among his best works, *The Gilded Age* (and especially its title) came to represent the entire post–Civil War era.

But for his greatest works, Twain would draw on his most familiar source: his boyhood home of Hannibal. His memories of Hannibal would first become the basis for the children's novel *The Adventures of Tom Sawyer* (1876). The story of a scheming, adventure-seeking boy much like Twain himself, *Tom Sawyer* introduced the characters and settings he would explore more fully in his masterpiece, *Adventures of Huckleberry Finn,* published in 1884.

Though based on his earlier children's novel and filled with his distinctive humor, *Huckleberry Finn* was perhaps Twain's most serious novel. As he traced the story of Huck—a poor, orphaned boy who helps a slave, Jim, escape his owner—Twain expressed his hatred of slavery, exposed the hypocrisies of

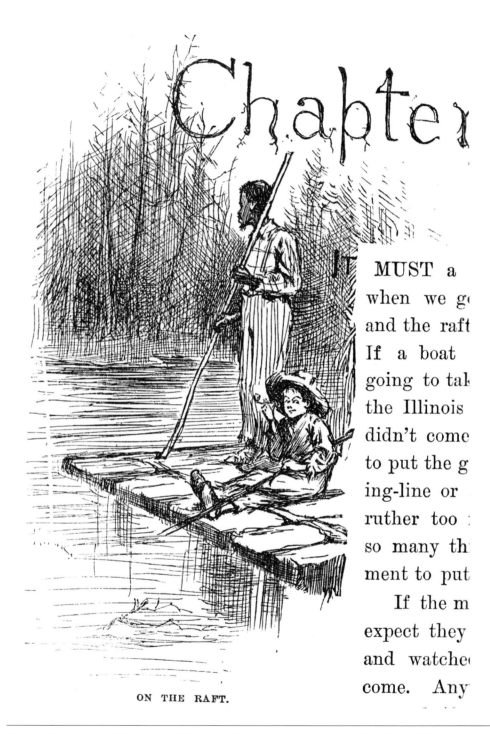

Chapter

IT MUST a
when we g
and the raft
If a boat
going to tak
the Illinois
didn't come
to put the g
ing-line or
ruther too
so many th
ment to put

If the m
expect they
and watche
come. Any

ON THE RAFT.

Twain's ideal of racial harmony: Huck and Jim floating down the Mississippi River.

American politics and culture, and recorded his respect for childhood innocence. Angry, nostalgic, and celebratory all at once, it is widely considered one of the very best American novels ever written, and its depiction of a boy and a slave rafting down the river to freedom remains one of the key images in American culture.

Twain would return to his childhood memories in his memoir, *Life on the Mississippi* (1883), to social satire in *A Connecticut Yankee at King Arthur's Court* (1889), and to the injustices of American race relations in *Pudd'nhead Wilson* (1894). But a series of failed business schemes, as well as a series of tragedies within his family, would strain his writing ability in his later years. Most of his later works were rushed to publication for financial reasons, and his output was uneven.

By the time he died in 1910, Twain was more famous as a wise and funny lecturer than as a great writer. In his increasingly familiar Southern drawl, Twain expressed his thoughts and impressions about a variety of subjects— often whatever popped into his head—to packed audiences around the world. Even audiences that had never read his books flocked to theaters to see him speak. But since then, critics, writers, and readers have confirmed what he always believed about himself: Mark Twain was one of the most original writers in modern literature.

William Dean Howells

Realist Novelist, Influential Editor

1837–1920

As a writer and editor of the late nineteenth century, William Dean Howells presided over a major change in American literature. Earlier novelists such as Nathaniel Hawthorne and Herman Melville explored philosophical ideas in stylized, often supernatural works. Others, including Susan Warner and Harriet Beecher Stowe, wrote sentimental novels that depended upon the heightened emotions of characters and readers for their effects. Almost none regarded their fiction as a kind of journalism. But Howells and the writers who followed him tried something new. By arguing for the careful observation of American life in his criticism and by objectively reporting on

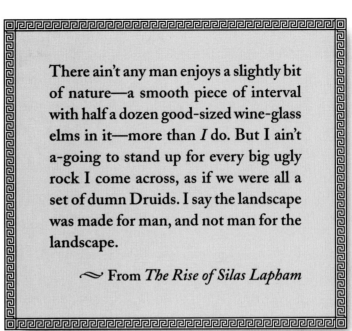

There ain't any man enjoys a slightly bit of nature—a smooth piece of interval with half a dozen good-sized wine-glass elms in it—more than *I* do. But I ain't a-going to stand up for every big ugly rock I come across, as if we were all a set of dumn Druids. I say the landscape was made for man, and not man for the landscape.

~ From *The Rise of Silas Lapham*

American society in his fiction, Howells ushered in the era of realism in American writing.

Howells was born in Martin's Ferry, Ohio, in 1837. His father, a printer and publisher, moved the family frequently in search of a market for his newspaper. Howells therefore received a meager formal education, but he did learn the journalist's trade at an early age. After turning nineteen, he left his father's business to work for newspapers in Cincinnati and Columbus, eventually becoming the editor of *The Ohio State Journal*.

His big break came in 1860, when he was selected by the Republican Party to write the official biography of its presidential candidate, Abraham Lincoln. As a reward for this work, he was appointed the American consul in Venice, Italy, after Lincoln's victory. In Italy he fulfilled his diplomatic duties and wrote several travel books. Then he returned to the United States in 1865 to become an editor, first at the *Nation,* one of the most important literary magazines in the country.

In 1871 he became editor of *The Atlantic Monthly,* another leading literary magazine, and for the next ten years was responsible for maintaining its quality and reputation. Among the writers he encouraged, edited, and published during this period were his friends Henry James and Mark Twain. Howells was also responsible for introducing American audiences to influential European writers such as Emile Zola, a French novelist who was championing the realistic description of everyday life in fiction. During these years, Howells published six novels in addition to a variety of articles, but it was not until he left his editorial position at *The Atlantic Monthly* in 1881 that he applied the new theories of realism to his own work.

A Modern Instance, his 1882 novel about a couple in the midst of a divorce, broke new ground in American literature. As the first novel to explore divorce honestly, without condemning either side, it offered a way for other writers to discuss the more serious issues of modern life. He followed it with the novel generally considered to be his realist masterpiece, *The Rise of Silas Lapham* (1885). The story of an enterprising man from a small town who becomes a leading paint manufacturer but finds that he can never become a member of elite society, *The Rise of Silas Lapham* provided one of the first positive depictions of modern business practices in American fiction.

In 1886, Howells moved to New York City to become a regular contributor to *Harper's Magazine.* From this post, he endorsed the careers of young writers such as Stephen Crane and Edith Wharton, wrote influential books about literature including 1891's *Criticism and Fiction,* and investigated the radical workers' rights and socialist movements of the era. These movements inspired many of his later works, including *A Hazard of New Fortunes* (1890), in which the economic struggle between employers and workers disrupts the operations of a popular New York magazine.

Late in life, Howells served as the first president of the American Academy of Arts and Letters. The 1908 appointment only made official what had been true for decades: Howells was a national literary ambassador. By the time he died in 1920, many writers had surpassed Howells in their skill for writing realistic fiction and in their willingness to explore the more scandalous aspects of American society. But all of them, from the ones he helped directly to the generations that followed, owed him a great debt for his innovations and for helping to modernize American literature.

Henry James

Writer of Psychological Novels and Short Stories
1843–1916

enry James grew up in one of the most important households in American cultural history. His father, Henry James Sr., taught all the James children to value intellectual pursuits over business concerns and to explore their own minds before they explored the rest of the world. As a result, Henry's older brother William became a prominent psychologist and one of the leading philosophers of the late nineteenth and early twentieth centuries. And

Henry became the premier writer of psychological novels in American literature.

Born on April 15, 1843, in New York City, Henry James spent much of his childhood in Europe, moving in and out of boarding schools as his father pursued new intellectual challenges

> In Geneva, as he had been perfectly aware, a young man wasn't at liberty to speak to a young unmarried lady save under certain rarely-occurring conditions; but here at Vevey what conditions could be better than these?—a pretty American girl coming to stand in front of you in a garden with all the confidence in life.
>
> ~ From *Daisy Miller*

and experiences. As a result of this lifestyle, he would never feel entirely comfortable in the nation of his birth and would always consider Europe a more complicated and stimulating place than the United States. He settled in Rhode Island in 1860, a year before the first shots were fired at Fort Sumter, igniting the Civil War. Though he was the right age for enlistment in the Union army, he was sickly, disinterested in physical pursuits, and ultimately rejected because of a back injury. Unable to participate directly in the events that would occupy the next five years of American history, James retreated into his own imagination, embarking on a career as a writer of articles and short stories for American magazines.

In 1876, after several additional visits to Europe and dozens of meetings with the most important writers of the era, he settled in London, a city with an old and complex culture. From London he began the detailed analysis of American society that would occupy him for the rest of his life. Several of his early works showed promise, including the 1876 novel *Roderick Hudson*. But it was not until the popular success of the short novel *Daisy Miller* (1878) that he found both a subject and a writing style suitable to his interests. The story of a wealthy, innocent American woman who tragically misunderstands European culture, *Daisy Miller* provided James and his readers with an opportunity to contrast New World and Old World customs. His next major work, *The Portrait of a Lady* (1881), developed this theme in greater detail and ranks among the very best novels of the nineteenth century. In his account of Isabel Archer's confrontation with English and Italian societies, James seemed to reach the height of his literary powers. But he was not content to repeat the style and plotline of these popular novels for the rest of his career.

In the second phase of his work, which lasted until the turn of the century, he experimented with increasingly subtle, psychologically detailed portraits of his characters. Long stories such as "The Aspern Papers" (1888) and "The Turn of the Screw" (1898), a Gothic tale about haunted children and their equally disturbed governess, set new standards for realistic fiction. Rich in analysis and description instead of action, they opened up new possibilities for James, allowing him to describe his characters' thoughts with greater nuance and precision.

His third phase, beginning in the early 1900s, combined the lessons he learned during the first two. In his last novels, *The Wings of the Dove* (1902), *The Ambassadors* (1903), and *The Golden Bowl* (1904)—each more dense and detailed than the last—he returned to his examination of American culture and explored the minute differences in thought that separated Americans from Europeans.

Throughout his career, James wrote influential essays about literature. He also tried his hand as a playwright. But it was as a writer of challenging fiction that he earned the respect and admiration of Americans and, more important to him, Europeans. In the final years of his life, James became increasingly impatient with his native land. During the early stages of World War I, he berated the American government for refusing to enter the war in support of its British allies. In 1915 he renounced the United States entirely and became a British citizen.

In January 1916, the English king awarded him an Order of Merit in recognition of his lifetime of literary achievement. A month later Henry James died, leaving behind a body of work that had stretched the limits of fiction and provided future writers with new strategies for realistic description. Encouraged at an early age to explore the life of the mind, Henry James did more than any other American writer to make that life available to readers and writers alike. In the process, he helped to define the most distinguishing features of nineteenth- and early-twentieth-century American culture for American and European audiences.

Kate Chopin

Feminist Writer Best Known for The Awakening
1851–1904

Early-twentieth-century champions of women's rights often faced hostile resistance. Many Americans feared that the feminists' calls for sexual equality would endanger family relationships and undermine society. Kate Chopin, author of the early feminist novel *The Awakening*, was a particularly unfortunate victim of their distrust.

Born Katherine O'Flaherty in 1851, Chopin was a child of privilege. Her father was an Irish immigrant who became a prosperous merchant in St. Louis, Missouri, and a founder of the Pacific Railroad. Her mother was a member of a prominent family from the French-Creole community of St. Louis. Poised between these two worlds, Katherine married Oscar Chopin, the wealthy son of a former Louisiana slaveholder, in 1870. A Creole businessman and owner of a cotton processing business, Chopin led his wife back to

> With a writhing motion she settled herself more securely in the hammock. She perceived that her will had blazed up, stubborn and resistant. She could not at that moment have done other than denied and resisted.
>
> ∼ From *The Awakening*

his home in New Orleans, Louisiana, where her unconventional habits shocked the local communities. Rejecting some of the limitations placed upon women in that setting, she smoked cigarettes, walked through the city streets without male accompaniment, and supported local artists. Despite these daring choices, the Chopins became central figures in New Orleans culture. Together they raised six children.

After Oscar died in 1882, Kate took her children back to St. Louis. To help herself cope with Oscar's death and to earn some much-needed money, she began to write about her Louisiana experiences. Throughout the 1880s and 1890s, she wrote a series of well-received short stories in the "local color" style so popular during that period. Such stories described unusual social and cultural practices from different parts of the country. Though many of Chopin's stories challenged the institution of marriage and questioned women's limited role in society, they were so entertaining and skillfully composed that critics were able to ignore these early hints of feminism. Soon Chopin was hosting a regular meeting of St. Louis literary figures, known as a salon, and rising to prominence in southern and midwestern intellectual circles. But her finest and most explicitly feminist novel, 1899's *The Awakening*, put an end to that rise.

The Awakening details a few months in the life of Edna Pontellier, a native of Kentucky who lives with her Creole husband in Louisiana. A social outsider, an uninterested mother, and a halfhearted wife, she is dissatisfied with her life until she falls in love with a younger man, Robert Lebrun. Over time, her love for Robert inspires her to change her life; she becomes an artist and ignores her responsibilities as a wife and mother. Finding little support for her new feelings in the Creole community—in which the roles of wife and mother were the only ones available to women—she decides to live entirely on her own. Awakened to her own desires, she nevertheless finds that her newfound freedom brings only loneliness and tragedy.

In its depiction of a woman unhappy with the role society had chosen for her, *The Awakening* broke new ground in American literature. Few books had ever dealt with women's feelings so openly and truthfully. For this reason, it met stiff opposition. Critics disapproved of the book and accused Chopin of immorality. And even though Chopin received letters of appreciation from sympathetic women around the country, she was shunned from many of the social circles that once welcomed her.

Chopin's literary output diminished after the controversy over *The Awakening*. When she died five years later, in 1904, her reputation seemed ruined forever. But in the 1960s and 1970s, the women's rights movement resurrected her novel as an early representation of women's complicated feelings, a major work in women's history, and a true gem of American literature.

Booker T. Washington

African American Educator, Memoirist
1856–1915

ooker T. Washington achieved a stature in American society that seemed impossible for a black man born into slavery in Franklin County, Virginia in 1856. A child when the Civil War ended in 1865, Washington spent the greater part of his life a freeman. However, young African Americans like Washington continued to face severely limited opportunities,

> I said that the whole future of the Negro rested largely upon the question as to whether or not he should make himself, through his skill, intelligence and character, of such undeniable value to the community in which he lived that the community could not dispense with his presence.
>
> ~ From *Up from Slavery*

despite the emancipation of the slaves after the war. In his teens, Washington worked a variety of jobs involving hard labor and could not have predicted that he would one day be the most famous African American writer and speaker in the nation.

Despite the hardships he faced in segregated America, Washington pieced together an education when he was not working. In 1872 he earned admission to Hampton Normal and Agricultural Institute in Virginia (now Hampton University), one of the first institutions of higher learning to service former slaves. He graduated in 1875 and, after brief stints as a teacher and as a student at a Baptist seminary, returned to Hampton as an instructor in 1879. Samuel Chapman Armstrong, the founder of Hampton, was so impressed with Washington's drive that he asked the young teacher to help him open a school for African Americans in Tuskegee, Alabama. The Tuskegee Normal and Industrial Institute, founded in 1881, became the base for Washington's rise to fame.

At Tuskegee, Washington devised a curriculum based on professional training and technical knowledge. He also taught his students the practical skills they would need in order to find jobs after emancipation, and hoped this strategy would prepare them for the economic challenges they faced. Many

African Americans supported these methods because they promised financial stability; many white Americans supported these methods because they ensured that African Americans would continue to be workers instead of cultural or political leaders. White politicians were particularly impressed with Washington's work after he delivered a speech in Atlanta in 1895 that detailed his plan for the gradual development of racial equality. But this speech also enraged a number of younger black intellectuals including W. E. B. Du Bois, who demanded an immediate recognition of racial equality and would become Washington's most influential opponent.

Washington wrote or cowrote a number of articles, biographies, and histories, but his most important literary work was *Up from Slavery* (1901). A memoir intended for white audiences, it emphasized the importance of hard work and patience in Washington's own rise to fame and importance. Unlike Du Bois's response in *The Souls of Black Folk* (1903), it did not openly criticize white prejudice or demand that African American men be allowed to vote, as was their Constitutional right. It even discouraged the inclusion of the arts in African American education. Nevertheless, it subtly suggested that racism was undermining American society and provided practical solutions to a problem that seemed insurmountable.

By issuing only modest demands for the black community, Washington set white politicians at ease. He was therefore admitted into the very center of American politics after the publication of the 1895 speech and *Up from Slavery*, befriending Presidents William McKinley and Theodore Roosevelt. But he did not abandon militant politics entirely; secretly he organized more radical demonstrations against racial oppression without attracting suspicion. Washington's strategy of accommodation allowed him to manipulate racial politics from the inside and from the outside of the American political mainstream.

But most Americans saw only the accommodating and modest approach detailed in works such as *Up from Slavery*. While this strategy may have made him the most prominent black speaker and writer of his era, it may also have undermined his ultimate goal of racial equality. Later black activists would not accept economic self-reliance as the only goal of the Civil Rights struggle; they would follow Du Bois's lead and demand immediate equality as well. And Washington, who prepared an entire generation of African Americans for the harsh realities of a segregated nation, would seem the more old-fashioned of the two intellectuals.

Owen Wister

Creator of the Modern Western
1860–1938

Owen Wister was not a cowboy. He was a talented but troubled member of the Mid-Atlantic elite, a child of wealth and privilege, and a lawyer by trade. He nevertheless popularized the image of the cowboy in American culture and wrote the first modern Western, *The Virginian,* generating a uniquely American literary genre.

Born on July 14, 1860, in Germantown, Pennsylvania, Wister was the only child of a Philadelphia doctor, Owen Jones Wister, and

> His broad soft hat was pushed back; a loose-knotted, dull-scarlet handkerchief sagged from his throat, and one casual thumb was hooked in the cartridge-belt that slanted across his hips. He had plainly come many miles from somewhere across the vast horizon, as the dust upon him showed.
>
> ～ From *The Virginian*

Sarah Butler Wister, a gifted musician with literary aspirations. His maternal grandmother, Fanny Kemble, was a famous Shakespearean actor and writer. Young Owen thus grew up in an intellectually challenging, artistic environment. Sadly, it was also a troubled environment. Both his parents suffered from psychological instability, and Wister too would fight mental illness for much of his life. To some extent, his sickness limited the extent of his literary production; but, indirectly, it also led him to his greatest subject matter.

Wister spent much of his childhood in boarding schools in America and Europe. The one constant in his early life was his love of music. Despite his father's discouragement, he was determined to pursue a career as a composer. After graduating with high honors from Harvard University in 1882, he studied music among the European masters. He also devoted some of his time to fiction writing. But in the end, his father convinced him to seek a more conventional profession.

Discouraged by his career change and disappointed that his earliest literary attempts had been failures, Wister suffered his first collapse in 1885. His doctor recommended that he recuperate in a warmer, more peaceful climate, so Wister made his first trip to Wyoming. It was a trip that would change his life.

Frederic Remington's illustrations, which often accompanied Wister's *Harper's Magazine* stories, helped define the image of the cowboy in American culture.

Although he would earn a law degree at Harvard over the next three years, he insisted on returning to Wyoming each summer and was more enthusiastic about his experiences on the Western ranches than about his actual job. Even after he earned a position at a Philadelphia law firm in 1890, he continued to daydream about the cowboys he met. And instead of practicing law, Wister spent most of his time locked in his office, writing fictional accounts of his days in Wyoming.

By 1893, *Harper's Magazine* was publishing Wister's stories, along with illustrations by the most celebrated painter of Western scenes, Frederic Remington. At the same time, Wister renewed his friendship with a Harvard classmate and fellow champion of the West, Theodore Roosevelt, the future twenty-sixth president of the United States. Wister's friendships with Remington and Roosevelt fed his interest in cowboys and inspired more stories and essays.

In 1901, Wister began collecting his best stories and reshaping them into a novel, *The Virginian: A Horseman of the Plains.* Describing the adventures of the title character, whose sharp instincts and honesty make him a natural leader among ranch hands, *The Virginian* celebrates a cowboy lifestyle that was already gone by the time the novel was published in 1902, replaced by corporate ranching and fenced-in lands. Nevertheless, Wister's depiction of the cowboy proved to be enormously seductive, and *The Virginian* became a best-seller. It introduced or popularized most of the elements of the modern Western: the tall, quiet, strong-willed hero; the violent code of ethics; the vigilante justice; the bond between man and horse. Unfortunately, it also revealed Wister's cultural and racial prejudices: He deliberately excluded minorities from his novel—though minorities actually represented a large proportion of actual cowboys—and he limited the roles of women. In this way, he helped to create the false impression that all cowboys were white men, an impression that endures in most Hollywood depictions of the Wild West.

After the success of *The Virginian,* Wister devoted more of his time to the political work he introduced, subtly, in the novel. Most frequently, he called for greater restrictions on immigration and minority activities and joined several organizations devoted to those issues. His racist brand of politics also infiltrated his later fiction, including his 1906 novel *Lady Baltimore,* as well as his subsequent essays.

His later life was interrupted by frequent bouts of mental illness. By the time he died on July 21, 1938, he had suffered several severe breakdowns. Yet he managed to participate in national politics and write until the end of his life. And he lived to see the genre he mastered, the Western, find new audiences with the advent of motion pictures. There have been five movie versions of *The Virginian* alone, as well as a popular 1960s television series adaptation. And *The Virginian* is still the most frequently imitated novel in American literature.

Edith Wharton

Novelist of New York's High Society
1862–1937

Like the European society it copied, the elite society of late-nineteenth- and early-twentieth-century New York was a complicated world of subtle relationships and strict moral codes. No writer reproduced this world as skillfully or as completely as one of its own members, Edith Wharton. Though Wharton was praised for the range and variety of stories she was able to produce in a career that spanned over forty years, it was as an observer of the

Manhattan elite that she wrote her finest novels and made her greatest mark on American literature.

Born Edith Newbold Jones in 1862 in New York City, Wharton was the daughter of a fashionable, influential couple. She was taught by her mother to value social connections and the trappings of wealth, and by her

> The glow of the stones warmed Lily's veins like wine. More completely than any other expression of wealth they symbolized the life she longed to lead, the life of fastidious aloofness and refinement in which every detail should have the finish of a jewel, and the whole form a harmonious setting to her own jewel-like rareness.
>
> ~ From *The House of Mirth*

father to value literature. Educated at home and abroad, she was raised to be a socialite. Her primary goal was to marry into a family as prominent as hers. Unfortunately, she was not suited to marry the man who became her husband in 1885, Edward Wharton.

The Whartons had very little in common. To escape the unhappiness of her marriage, Edith Wharton resurrected an early interest in writing. Initially a poet, she began experimenting with fiction. In time, she was writing and publishing short stories that garnered high praise, particularly when they were collected and published in the 1899 volume *The Greater Inclination*. Encouraged by the success of her first volume of fiction—whose stories covered such diverse subjects as social manners, supernatural encounters, and theories about artistic creation—she dedicated more of her time and energy to her writing career.

She wrote several more short stories, collected in the 1904 volume *The Descent of Man*, as well as a novel about eighteenth-century Italy before publishing her first major contribution to American literature, *The House of Mirth* (1905). With this novel, Wharton followed the advice of her novelist friend Henry James and wrote about the New York society she knew best. The story of Lily Bart, a beautiful socialite whose marriage plans are disrupted by her father's bankruptcy and death, *The House of Mirth* revealed the secret negotiations of Manhattan's most influential families. Through her rich, incisive prose, Wharton illustrated the importance of personal reputations—particularly the reputations of women—in elite society and exposed the ease with which such reputations are made and ruined. An American literary phenomenon, it sold more than 100,000 copies in its first two months.

After the publication of *The House of Mirth,* Wharton separated from her husband and moved to Paris, the city that became her permanent home. She published her second major novel, *Ethan Frome* in 1911. Despite the distance between her new home and her native land, *Ethan Frome* delved even deeper into the American landscape than her previous works, with equally startling effects. Set in turn-of-the-century New England, *Ethan Frome* is the story of an inarticulate man who is trapped in a difficult marriage and, tragically, falls in love with a younger woman. As astute about the social values of a rural community as *The House of Mirth* had been about urban values, *Ethan Frome* proved Wharton's versatility and her mastery of the modern American novel.

In 1913, Wharton divorced her husband; she remained in Paris to continue her writing career. Later her apartment became a meeting place, or salon, for many of the most talented artists and intellectuals who were flocking to the French capital during and after World War I, including Americans Ernest Hemingway and F. Scott Fitzgerald. She also began publishing at an accelerated pace. She produced several volumes of short stories, several books supporting the Allied forces during World War I, and two brilliant novels that revisited and improved upon the themes of *The House of Mirth: The Custom of the Country* (1913), in which an ambitious woman rises to the top of New York society, and *The Age of Innocence* (1920), for which she won the 1921 Pulitzer Prize. *The Age of Innocence* is the story of a Manhattan socialite doomed to a life of unhappiness by her marriage to an untrustworthy Polish count and of the young New York lawyer who loves her; with that book Wharton reached the apex of her descriptive power as well as of her ability to reproduce the complex social networks of her parents' world.

Through the 1920s and 1930s, Wharton wrote in a variety of genres. *Old New York,* a 1924 compilation of four novelettes about New York City in the nineteenth century, earned particular praise among critics. Her writer's manual, *The Writing of Fiction* (1925), and her autobiography, *A Backward Glance* (1934), also proved popular and influential. But by the late 1930s, Wharton's work seemed old-fashioned in both style and subject matter. Even before she died in 1937, she was considered a figure from the literary past.

Since her death, Wharton's reputation has improved dramatically, and through several movie adaptations of her novels, she has been reintroduced to popular audiences. By combining the two major themes of her personal life—her membership in the New York aristocracy and her unhappy marriage—Wharton produced novels and short stories that dissected American social norms and pushed the limits of American fiction. She is now considered one of the most significant novelists in American literary history.

W.E.B. Du Bois

Civil Rights Activist, Historian, Social Theorist
1868–1963

An innovator of literature, sociology, and politics, W. E. B. Du Bois is now recognized as one of the most important figures in American history. His work laid the foundations for the Civil Rights movement as well as for the artistic innovations of the Harlem Renaissance. In his writings and through his political activities, he fought for the poor and oppressed of all nations. And by his own actions, he proved the equality of the races at a time when the United States was just recovering from the effects of slavery.

William Edward Burghardt Du Bois did not live the typical life of an African American in the era after the Civil War. He grew up in Great Barrington, Massachusetts, where racism was less pronounced than in other regions, and he received a fine education. Intelligent and motivated, he graduated from high school at sixteen and earned a scholarship to Fisk University in Nashville, Tennessee. During the summers, he taught in the local black communities around Fisk and, for the first time, observed the bitter struggle of the former slaves, who were shunned, abused, and even lynched by white neighbors. These experiences convinced Du Bois that he had important work to do as a champion of African American rights.

After graduating from Fisk in 1888, he won a scholarship to the graduate school at Harvard University. Seven years later, he became the first African American to receive a doctorate degree from Harvard. As a college educator, he focused primarily on black history and sociology. His influential research on the economic and cultural effects of slavery on black communities earned him teaching positions at Wilberforce University in Ohio and Atlanta University in Georgia. From these posts, he became a leading intellectual and advocate for African American rights.

> The problem of the twentieth century is the problem of the color line—the relation of the darker to the lighter races of men in Asia and Africa, in America and the islands of the sea.
>
> ~ From *The Souls of Black Folk*

In 1903 he compiled some of his early writings into the most important book of his career, *The Souls of Black Folk*. An analysis of black history, music, and culture, *The Souls of Black Folk* addressed the plight of African Americans from a variety of angles. Most important, Du Bois opposed racism by celebrating the cultural and intellectual achievements of the African American community, including the music of the slave spirituals. He argued that such achievements proved the equality of African Americans, and he demanded that American society recognize that equality immediately. In this way, he rejected the more gradual drift toward equality advocated by the most prominent black leader at the turn of the century, Booker T. Washington. And he inspired a younger generation of black writers, artists, and musicians, who would gather in the Harlem section of Manhattan in the 1920s to share ideas and re-create the African American culture of earlier generations for the twentieth century. This movement is now known as the Harlem Renaissance.

Two years after publishing *The Souls of Black Folk,* Du Bois entered the political battle for equality in a more dramatic way, by helping to organize the Niagara Movement, a convention of black leaders. The convention ultimately laid the groundwork for the National Association for the Advancement of Colored People (NAACP), one of the leading civil rights organizations in American history. At its founding in 1910, Du Bois was elected an officer of the association as well as the editor of its journal, *The Crisis.*

During the next thirty years, Du Bois would continue his activism, despite paying a heavy price for his views. His unflinching desire for an immediate end to all racial oppression, in the United States as well as in other countries, ultimately spoiled his relationship with the NAACP and cost him his position at Atlanta University. He published several highly influential books during this period—including a collection of controversial essays, *Darkwater* (1920); a history of the black experience after slavery, *Black Reconstruction in the South* (1935); and an autobiography, *Dusk of Dawn* (1940)—but his political battles increasingly occupied his attention. He opposed the European colonization of Africa and, after World War II, the proliferation of nuclear weapons around the world.

During the cold war of the 1950s, when tensions between the United States and the Soviet Union were at their height, the U.S. government often questioned and even harassed its critics. Du Bois became one of its primary targets. His visits to the Soviet Union and China, America's primary rivals, did little to help his reputation. In 1961, after losing several battles with the federal government, he moved to the African nation of Ghana. Two years later he became a citizen of that nation. The leaders of Ghana organized a hero's funeral for Du Bois after he died, on August 27, 1963. Sadly, the United States, which was in the midst of the Civil Rights movement Du Bois helped to create, paid less attention. At that time he was still considered a dangerous figure in his native land.

As a scholar, an editor, a politician, and a writer, Du Bois exerted a tremendous influence on African American history in particular and on American history in general. *The Souls of Black Folk* alone would have made his reputation as a ground-breaking intellectual and an inspiration to generations of black cultural figures. But over the course of his long life, Du Bois amassed an enormous body of work, both literary and political, rivaling that of any other twentieth-century figure. Americans could not ignore his work forever. Indeed, since the end of the Civil Rights movement, his contributions have received the attention they deserve in the country he fought so hard to change.

Stephen Crane

Realist Novelist, Wartime Reporter
1871–1900

Famous for his honest depictions of life's harsh realities, Stephen Crane pursued adventure and danger in part to improve his fiction. But the reckless, combative approach to life that made Crane a literary innovator and a unique voice in nineteenth-century fiction also contributed to the premature conclusion of his writing career and his early death.

Crane was born in Newark, New Jersey, on November 1, 1871. His father was a Methodist minister; his mother wrote articles about religious matters and worked for a variety of charitable organizations. Stephen was their fourteenth child and almost certainly their most rebellious. Attracted to the very activities his parents despised—including gambling, fighting, and drinking—he was sent to a military school as a teenager. Later he attended Lafayette

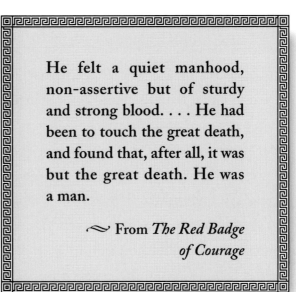

He felt a quiet manhood, non-assertive but of sturdy and strong blood. . . . He had been to touch the great death, and found that, after all, it was but the great death. He was a man.

⌁ From *The Red Badge of Courage*

College in Pennsylvania, where he studied mining engineering.

Crane was easily distracted and often divided his energies among a number of undertakings. Throughout his scholastic career, he worked as a reporter for one of his brothers, who owned a press bureau. And when he was not reporting, he was seeking other, less wholesome experiences. His studies suffered as a result. He failed out of Lafayette and only attended Syracuse University for a brief time. Determined to escape his parents' comfortable lifestyle, he finally settled in the Bowery section of New York City, one of the city's roughest and poorest neighborhoods, where he reported for *The New York Tribune.*

In the Bowery, he completed a novella about life in the slums, *Maggie: A Girl of the Streets,* in 1893. A realistic portrayal of an uneducated, unsophisticated young woman who struggles to escape her family's poverty by becoming a prostitute, it was too explicit for most readers of the 1890s, and the book sold poorly. His next novel, however, *The Red Badge of Courage* (1895), made him famous. The story of Henry Fielding, a Civil War soldier who wrestles with his fears and doubts as a battle rages around him, *The Red Badge of Courage* depicted the war in a new way. Unlike previous novels that celebrated the courage and heroism of the soldiers, Crane's novel—which he based on newspaper research rather than firsthand combat experience—explored the moral questions that war raised and the psychological effects it had on combatants. Together, *Maggie* and *The Red Badge of Courage* helped to usher in a new era of gritty, realistic writing that ignored the genteel standards that had dominated American literature.

After the success of his second novel, Crane traveled the country as a journalist and published fiction as well as poetry. But his work during this period failed to fulfill the expectations he set with his first two novels. In 1897 he moved to England, which became his base of operations as he reported on several international wars—including the Greco-Turkish War of 1897 and the Spanish-American War of 1898—for American newspapers. Some of his experiences provided material for fiction, including an 1897 shipwreck near Cuba that he would fictionalize in one of his greatest short stories, "The Open Boat."

But his reckless lifestyle sapped both his writing and his strength. After a long battle with tuberculosis, the adventurous writer died in Germany at the age of 28, leaving behind a small body of daring, realistic fiction that impressed several of his contemporaries—especially William Dean Howells—and would have a tremendous influence on future American writers such as Ernest Hemingway and Norman Mailer.

Theodore Dreiser

Naturalist Novelist, Social Critic
1871–1945

Theodore Dreiser was born in a small town—Terre Haute, Indiana—to German immigrant parents who struggled financially and could not support their ten children. He was an outsider from the very beginning: isolated, impoverished, and inexperienced in the very center of America's heartland. Like the characters of his later fiction, however, he dreamed of leading an important, influential

> She was sad beyond measure, and yet uncertain, wishing, fancying. Finally, it seemed as if all her state was one of loneliness and forsakenness, and she could scarce refrain from trembling at the lip. She hummed and hummed as the moments went by . . . and was therein as happy though she did not perceive it, as she ever would be.
>
> ∼ From *Sister Carrie*

life. And like those characters, he left his humble origins for the promise of the big city.

When Dreiser first arrived in Chicago, he was fifteen years old and forced to work a series of menial jobs to survive. Despite the hardships of urban living, he valued his freedom. After a short stay at Indiana University—a supportive schoolteacher offered to pay his tuition—he returned to Chicago, determined to achieve financial stability on his own. In 1892 he found a job as a cub reporter for a daily newspaper. The work appealed to him; newspaper writing brought him closer to the important events of his era. During the following decade, he took jobs with several midwestern newspapers, learning his craft, before accepting an editorial position at a New York magazine.

In New York, Dreiser proved especially skillful as a writer of feature articles. Recognizing the relationship between good features and good fiction, he began experimenting with short stories. In 1899 he started his first novel, writing its title, "Sister Carrie," on a sheet of paper and then drafting a story to fit the title. The result was one of his most important works, the first great American novel of the twentieth century.

Sister Carrie (1900) describes an affair between a married man, George Hurstwood, and a midwestern girl, Carrie Meeber, who has already lost her innocence by living with a traveling salesman in Chicago. Together they flee to New York, where Hurstwood suffers a series of emotional and financial setbacks while Carrie fulfills her dreams and rises to prominence as a Broadway actress. Dreiser's initial readers were shocked that Carrie is never punished for her affairs, and his publishers discontinued the book to quiet the outcry. Nevertheless, *Sister Carrie* announced Dreiser's arrival as an important new writer of the naturalist school, one who tried to describe the social forces influencing his characters without judging his characters' actions.

Supporting himself as a magazine editor for the next ten years, Dreiser worked on his second novel, *Jennie Gerhardt* (1911), another exploration of marital infidelity. He also planned the Cowperwood trilogy—*The Financier* (1912), *The Titan* (1914), and *The Stoic* (1947)—a sweeping critique of American business that examined in greater detail the political ideas he first explored in *Sister Carrie*. He continued these investigations in his 1915 novel about the exploitation of artists and writers, *The "Genius."* And then he combined the lessons he learned from each of these studies to produce his crowning achievement, the 1925 novel *An American Tragedy*. Based on the true story of a 1906 murder, *An American Tragedy* recounts the sad life of Clyde Griffiths, a poor boy who aspires to wealth and fame but kills his girlfriend when she becomes an obstacle to his rise. The pinnacle of Dreiser's naturalist style, the novel blames America's obsessions with money and status as much as Griffiths's own weaknesses for the murder. It achieved a level of popularity and success previously unknown to Dreiser, and it was quickly adapted for the stage and screen. Still, it did little to improve Dreiser's reputation among audiences critical of his realistic depictions of American life, and it was even banned in Boston in 1926.

In his later years, Dreiser negotiated movie contracts for several of his other works. He also used the success of *An American Tragedy* and his growing literary fame as a platform for his political ideas. Sympathetic to the plight of the poor since his own impoverished childhood, he was increasingly attracted to the revolutionary ideas of socialism and, later, communism. After visiting the Soviet Union to study its communist system, he returned to the United States to publish *Dreiser Looks at Russia* (1928). This book, a sympathetic portrait of the nation's enemy, along with his increasingly vocal criticisms of American business made him unpopular with the U.S. government. Over time, his reputation as a political radical overshadowed his reputation as a writer. Nevertheless, Dreiser professed his revolutionary beliefs for the rest of his life, and even joined the Communist Party before his death in 1945.

Theodore Dreiser was not the most skillful or poetic novelist of his era. He may not even have been the best storyteller. But he was among the most courageous. At a time when American writers were avoiding difficult social issues—infidelity, crime, murder, exploitation—Dreiser based his career on them. As a result, he forced American writers to take a closer, more honest look at the society surrounding them and to write more truthfully in the hope of describing the country more accurately.

Willa Cather

Writer Best Known for Great Plains Novels
1873–1947

*L*ike the home-steaders depicted in her fiction, Willa Cather turned the raw material of the American West into something new and unique. Her novels about life at the edge of American society countered the popular image of the cowboy with a new kind of hero: the strong-willed woman who fought to keep her family alive. In the process, Cather became one of America's most distinct novelists—a brilliant historian of the American West as

> There was nothing but land: not a country at all, but the material out of which countries are made. No, there was nothing but land . . . I had the feeling that the world was left behind, that we had got over the edge of it, and were outside man's jurisdiction.
>
> ~ From *My Ántonia*

well as a precise observer of the national character.

Willa Cather was born in Winchester, Virginia, in 1873, into a family with deep ties to the South. In 1883 the Cathers left their ancestral home for the Great Plains, following vast migrations of Americans seeking opportunity on the western frontier. They settled in Red Cloud, Nebraska, a town of regional significance because of its railroad station. The Cathers struggled financially in Nebraska. Willa was an unconventional figure in the conservative, business-minded environment of Red Cloud; she cut her hair unfashionably short, preferred to wear men's clothing, and dreamed of a literary life. Nevertheless, Cather succeeded academically in Red Cloud and enrolled at the University of Nebraska, in Lincoln, after high school. She studied journalism in college and published her first short stories, including one called "Peter," which would later provide the basis for her novel *My Ántonia*.

After graduation, she found a job as a magazine editor—and then a newspaper editor—in Pittsburgh, Pennsylvania. At the same time, she published stories in national magazines including *Cosmopolitan* and *McClure's Magazine*. Finding that her editorial duties interfered with her fiction writing—which was quickly becoming her primary concern—but still reluctant to rely on fiction for her living, she left editing to become a high-school teacher in 1901. While teaching, she published a volume of poetry and a short story collection, *The Troll Garden* (1905). She then returned to editing, this time for *McClure's Magazine* in New York. In addition to fulfilling her managing editor's duties at *McClure's*, she published her first novel, *Alexander's Bridge*, in 1912. Its success finally convinced Cather that she could survive on her fiction alone; the following year she gave up editorial work for good.

At the suggestion of Sarah Orne Jewett, a writer from Maine who had developed a reputation for novels set in remote, unfamiliar regions of the American landscape, Cather focused her attention on the Nebraska plains of her childhood. The immediate result of this new literary interest was *O Pioneers!*, her 1913 novel about a Norwegian immigrant, Alexandra Bergson, who sacrifices her own happiness in order to run her family's Nebraska farm and establish its financial security. Part tragedy, part celebration of American resilience, it suggested for the first time that the immigrant families of the heartland could be worthy and heroic subjects for American literature. Cather built upon this theme in her next two novels as well: *The Song of the Lark* (1915), about a Swedish immigrant who translates the musical culture of her midwestern town into a career as an international opera singer; and *My Ántonia* (1918), another portrait of an immigrant girl who bears the responsibility of her family's survival, and one of Cather's true masterpieces.

Cather continued to write about the harsh American West for the rest of her career and was eventually honored for her achievements with a variety of awards, including the 1923 Pulitzer Prize for her novel *One of Ours* (1922). But she also branched out into other subjects and experimented with new techniques, including a narrative style in which she focused almost entirely on the psychologies of single characters. The power and success of these later works varied, but among them was one of her finest, *Death Comes for the Archbishop*

(1927). Set in the Southwest in the 1840s and 1850s, *Death Comes for the Archbishop* detailed the work of Catholic missionaries living among Native American tribes. Like her previous novels, it described the modernization of western life. But it provided a spiritual as well as a physical context for the conflicts of modernization and served as a culmination of her analysis of westward expansion.

Cather wrote and published for another twenty years after *Death Comes for the Archbishop*. Her popularity, never dependent on a literary fashion or a "school" of writing, survived several shifts in American literary taste. But her reputation, before and after her death in 1947, was based on the brilliant portraits of life on the Great Plains that she wrote between 1913 and 1927. In these novels, the enterprising pioneers that she knew in her childhood became symbols of national perseverance. And her own strength and independence, when translated to the lives of her characters, came to represent the most celebrated aspects of the American character.

Robert Frost

Poet of Rural New England
1874–1963

obert Frost was one of the most popular poets of the twentieth century. With memorable works such as "Stopping by Woods on a Snowy Evening" and "The Road Not Taken," he earned a broad audience and a reputation for being the premier poet of New England life. His best poems were quickly considered classics of American literature. But he was more than the folksy peasant that was his popular image. He was a native Californian

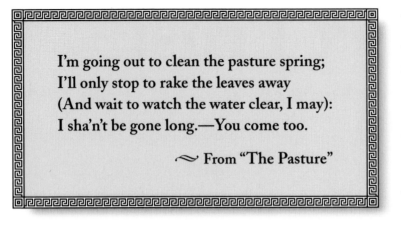

> I'm going out to clean the pasture spring;
> I'll only stop to rake the leaves away
> (And wait to watch the water clear, I may):
> I sha'n't be gone long.—You come too.
>
> ∼ From "The Pasture"

who made his home in New England, a farmer who studied and taught at the finest schools in the United States, a plain-spoken man who befriended the finest poets of Europe, and a writer of subtle, elegant, complicated poems.

Frost was born on March 26, 1874, in San Francisco, California. Named after Robert E. Lee, the leader of the Confederate armies during the Civil War, he was the son of a newspaper editor and Democratic politician. Following his father's death, eleven-year-old Frost; his younger sister, Jeanie; and his mother moved to New England to live with their extended family. Traveling from town to town in Massachusetts and New Hampshire, as his mother tracked down available teaching jobs, Frost received a sporadic education. In 1892, despite skipping entire grades as a child, he graduated at the top of his high-school class in Lawrence, Massachusetts and shared valedictory honors with a classmate who would soon become his wife, Elinor White.

After graduation he enrolled at Dartmouth College, but he did not complete his first semester. Restless and dissatisfied with academic life, Frost tried several occupations, working as a schoolteacher, a mill hand, and a newspaper reporter. He even published a few poems. By 1895 he was married and had a growing family to support, but he was still unable to find his way in the world. He decided to return to college and entered Harvard University in 1897. He withdrew again, this time after completing two full years of coursework, and transplanted his family to a working farm in Derry, New Hampshire. At night, when his farming chores were finished, Frost experimented with new forms of poetry, but he did not succeed in publishing much of his early work.

Nevertheless, Frost staked his future on his poems. In 1912—after leaving the Derry farm and returning to the classroom to teach for a few years—he sailed to England, settled in a cottage north of London, and concentrated all of his energies on his writing. The result, a volume called *A Boy's Will,* was published in London in 1913. *A Boy's Will* earned positive reviews and attracted the attention of influential writers such as Ezra Pound, who defended Frost's work to Europe's avant-garde literary communities. At first glance, Frost's poems seemed old-fashioned, featuring lyrical rhythms and standard rhyme schemes. Famously, they also mimicked the simple speech patterns of New England farmers. But Pound and others recognized in Frost's poems both a philosophical subtlety and an acute awareness of the power of language. Frost's depictions of country life contained bitter ironies; even his plainest poems hinged on moments of miscommunication and misunderstanding, suggesting that his simple farmers were less simple than they appeared.

A year later, Frost published *North of Boston,* an even more influential volume that featured some of his best work, including "Mending Wall," "The Mountain," and two of his most haunting poems, "The Death of the Hired Man" and "Home Burial." Finally a literary success, after almost twenty years of trial and error, Frost returned to the United States in 1915. At home in the Northeast, he developed a reputation as a popular lecturer and reader. He also accepted a series of university teaching assignments and continued to write acclaimed poems and several plays. He won four Pulitzer Prizes in the following years, for *New Hampshire* (1924), *Collected Poems* (1930), *A Further Range* (1936), and *A Witness Tree* (1942).

Robert Frost reads "The Gift Outright" at President John F. Kennedy's inauguration.

Although his later life was marred by personal tragedies—including the deaths of his sister, his wife, several of his children, and even grandchildren—he maintained his stature as the nation's most popular and important poet. Each generation seemed to discover Frost anew. He reached the widest audience of his career in 1961, when he read a poem, "The Gift Outright," at John F. Kennedy's presidential inauguration. In the final years of his life, at Kennedy's request, Frost embarked on a worldwide lecture tour, visiting Israel, Greece, and even the Soviet Union as a U.S. cultural ambassador. These trips enhanced his reputation abroad, but they took an enormous toll on his aging body. After a long period of illness, he died on January 29, 1963.

As a poet who achieved both critical and popular success in his own lifetime, Frost was unusual among the writers of the early twentieth century. He made complex ideas sound simple and, in the process, became one of the most beloved writers in American literary history.

Gertrude Stein

Experimental Writer, Patron of the Arts
1874–1946

Though Gertrude Stein remained an American citizen, she spent most of her life in Paris. Her apartment in that city, at 27 rue de Fleurus, was a center of artistic innovation in the early part of the twentieth century. Writers, painters, and musicians from Europe and America congregated there to trade ideas and receive encouragement from its famous residents, Stein and Alice B. Toklas, her secretary and partner. For the importance of her apartment alone,

Stein would have been famous. But she was also an influential writer, and her experimental works, such as the stories in *Three Lives* (1909) and the poems in *Tender Buttons* (1914), helped to shape the cosmopolitan, revolutionary kind of writing known as modernism, which dominated world literature in the 1920s, 1930s, and 1940s.

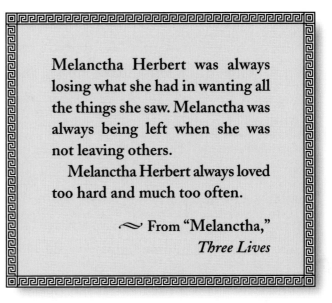

Melanctha Herbert was always losing what she had in wanting all the things she saw. Melanctha was always being left when she was not leaving others.

Melanctha Herbert always loved too hard and much too often.

～ From "Melanctha," *Three Lives*

Stein was born in Allegheny, Pennsylvania, in 1874 to German-Jewish immigrants. Her father was a successful businessman who moved his family frequently, and Stein spent much of her childhood in Europe. In 1893 she enrolled in Radcliffe College at Harvard University, where she studied with William James, a famous psychologist and brother of novelist Henry James. She then attended medical school at Johns Hopkins University but did not graduate. Instead she followed her brother Leo, an aspiring painter, to Paris in 1903.

Leo never succeeded with his own art. But with the money they inherited from their father, Gertrude and Leo became supporters of other young, avant-garde painters then living in Paris, including Pablo Picasso, Henri Matisse, and Juan Gris. They bought these artists' works and provided them with artistic and financial support. By the early 1920s, Gertrude was also attracting to the apartment a crowd of expatriate writers, including Ernest Hemingway, F. Scott Fitzgerald, and other Americans disillusioned by the recently concluded world war. She named this group the "lost generation."

As she was gathering the best writers and painters of the age to meet in her apartment, Stein was also mixing literary and painterly techniques in her own writing. In the short stories of *Three Lives,* for instance, she adapted the repetitious style of Picasso's cubist paintings and the boldness of Matisse's work to her storytelling. She introduced fragmented word patterns into her fiction and emphasized the psychology of her characters over plot development. Similarly, in the poetry of *Tender Buttons,* she began working with loose rhythms rather than obvious rhymes, and she practiced abstract descriptions rather than the traditional storyline development of most nineteenth- and early-twentieth-century poetry. She continued these and other experiments in her autobiographical 1925 novel, *The Making of Americans;* her autobiography entitled *The Autobiography of Alice B. Toklas* (1933); and even in her lyrics for the opera *Four Saints in Three Acts* (1934).

These works, as well as their conversations with Stein in Paris, inspired American writers such as Hemingway and Sherwood Anderson to create the literary styles—including their famously condensed, precise descriptions—that came to define American modernist literature. On her own as well as through her followers, Stein therefore commanded a major shift in the way people wrote and thought in the twentieth century.

With *The Autobiography of Alice B. Toklas,* Stein finally achieved popular recognition to go along with the acclaim she had already earned among writers and painters. After its publication, Stein returned to the United States in 1934 for a well-received lecture tour. It was her only visit to the United States after her 1903 move to Paris.

During World War II, as Germany invaded France, she turned her attention from writers and artists to the American soldiers who helped free Paris from

Nazi control. Her apartment became a center for servicemen in need of rest and comfort, and her writing, in 1945's *Wars I Have Seen* and 1946's *Brewsie and Willie*, celebrated the heroism of the troops she met and aided.

Stein died in 1946, having achieved lasting fame as a primary architect of a literary revolution as well as a reputation for producing some of the most challenging literature of her era.

Jack London

Writer of Popular Adventure Stories
1876–1916

Jack London was born in San Francisco in 1876 but spent his early childhood on the road, as his stepfather moved the family from one city to another following a series of unsuccessful business ventures. These early experiences set the pattern for the rest of his life. London would seldom stop moving, not even after he had achieved extraordinary fame as one of America's most popular writers and most interesting real-life characters.

After ten years of travel, London's family settled in Oakland, California in 1886. There, young Jack finally enjoyed some stability. He frequented the city library and, for a short time, owned his own boat and cruised San Francisco Bay illegally trolling for oysters. But by 1893, the seventeen-year-old was on the move again. First he signed on to a seven-month Pacific voyage on a sealing vessel. When he returned from this voyage, he worked in a mill and at a power plant for a street railway. He also participated in political demonstrations, joining a group of frustrated workingmen who were marching to Washington, D.C., to protest poor labor conditions. Never one to persist in a cause for long, he deserted this group before it reached the capital and then roamed the nation as a hobo until he was imprisoned for vagrancy in Buffalo, New York. In 1895, after two years of adventure, he returned to Oakland High School to prepare for his University of California entrance examinations. Accepted in 1896 he only stayed at the Berkeley campus for only one semester. Then he was off again on another adventure.

In the year that London entered college, prospectors discovered gold in the Klondike region of northwestern Canada, near the Alaskan border. The discovery attracted miners and risk takers from all over the world, who rushed

> When the long winter nights come on and the wolves follow their meat into the lower valleys, he may be seen running at the head of the pack . . . his great throat a-bellow as he sings a song of the younger world, which is the song of the pack.
>
> ∽ From *The Call of the Wild*

into this harsh climate and began a desperate search for precious metals. Young Jack London followed them. Like most of the gold rush hopefuls, however, London never found the fortune he dreamed about.

Returning empty-handed from the Klondike, London decided to devote the rest of his life to fiction writing. While he would continue to wander the globe—touring the United States as a lecturer for the Socialist Party and as a candidate for the Oakland mayoralty, visiting battlefields in South America and Asia as a war correspondent, and sailing to Europe and Australia during an ill-fated world cruise—the second half of London's life was organized around and sustained by his fiction.

By 1903, London had written his first best-seller, *The Call of the Wild,* the story of a California dog, Buck, who is kidnapped and shipped to Alaska to aid prospectors during the gold rush. As the savagery of the Alaskan environment transforms the once-docile Buck into the leader of a wild wolf pack, London reveals his favorite and most characteristic theme: the environment's effect in shaping and reshaping character. Three years later, he would return to this theme in *White Fang* (1906), in which a savage dog is tamed and civilized by a man's love. His 1904 bestseller, *The Sea-Wolf,* a novel based on his experiences on the sealing vessel, and several of his best short stories including "To Build a Fire" (1908) would also explore ideas about nature, civilization, and survival under harsh conditions. Like all of London's most characteristic writing, these stories identified the basic struggle between life and death that threatened even the most comfortable existence.

Despite his status as one of the nation's first millionaire writers, London amassed an enormous personal debt during his reckless adventures. In the last years of his life, he published an assortment of books and stories, but most were written only for cash and were not as highly regarded as his earlier work.

Besides his mounting debts, a variety of ailments—including alcoholism—and a series of family misfortunes plagued him until he died, on November 22, 1916, from an overdose of painkillers. The wandering lifestyle that provided material for his best stories also contributed to his early death, at the age of forty.

Upton Sinclair

Muckraking Novelist, Politician, Reformer
1878–1968

In the American tradition of political fiction—which includes works as influential as Harriet Beecher Stowe's antislavery novel, *Uncle Tom's Cabin,* and John Steinbeck's Depression epic, *The Grapes of Wrath*—few books have had as sudden and sweeping an impact as Upton Sinclair's *The Jungle.* But Sinclair's exposé of the meat-packing industry was only one example of the writer's social activism, one novel from a literary career that spanned over a half-century, produced more than eighty books, and extended into the contested areas of labor organization, Civil Rights work, and electoral politics.

Sinclair was born in Baltimore in 1878, but his parents were Virginia natives who lost their fortunes during the Civil War. Depressed by his losses and dependent on alcohol, his father moved the family to New York, where Upton grew up in

> Neither the squeals of hogs nor tears of visitors made any difference to them; one by one they hooked up the hogs, and one by one with a swift stroke they slit their throats. There was a long line of hogs, with squeals and lifeblood ebbing away together.
>
> ～ From *The Jungle*

a series of boarding houses among the impoverished and desperate he would later champion in his fiction. His first writing attempts were not politically motivated, however. After entering City College as a fourteen-year-old, Sinclair began writing popular children's stories, dime novels of action and adventure. He proved both imaginative and prolific.

By the turn of the century, he decided to concentrate more of his energies on serious fiction and penned several unsuccessful novels. He also discovered his political voice during this period while he worked as a reporter for newspapers supported by the Socialist Party. When he finally combined these interests, blending social activism and fiction in his 1906 novel *The Jungle,* he achieved financial success and lasting fame.

The Socialist Party had sent Sinclair to Chicago in 1904 to report on working conditions in the meat-packing industry. To his surprise, he found more than exploited workers during his tours. The unsanitary conditions in the packing plants posed a serious health risk to American consumers and horrified Sinclair. He wrote *The Jungle* in protest. The story of Jurgis Rudkus, a Lithuanian immigrant struggling to survive in the New World, *The Jungle* was a sprawling novel about the lives of the urban poor. But the scenes based on Sinclair's observations of the meat-packing industry were the ones that left a lasting impression on readers. The classic novel of the muckraking tradition, whose primary purpose was to expose political and industrial corruption, it alerted Americans to the dangers of the food supply. It even shocked President Theodore Roosevelt, who after reading Sinclair's work threw his support behind the Food and Drug Act of 1906, which authorized government oversight of food and drug manufacturing.

Sinclair followed the blockbuster success of *The Jungle* with exposés of the coal industry in *King Coal* (1917) and the oil industry in *Oil!* (1927), among other muckraking novels. He also helped organize labor unions, engaged in public protests, helped to found the American Civil Liberties Union, and continued to participate in Socialist politics as a writer and campaigner.

After thirty years of work, he left the Socialist Party in 1934. During that same year, he earned the Democratic Party's nomination to run for governor of California. He lost a close election, but the success of his campaign—based on the slogan "End Poverty in California," or "EPIC"—inspired other Democratic politicians, including President Franklin D. Roosevelt, to seek more radical solutions to the problems of the Great Depression.

Through the 1940s, Sinclair wrote a series of popular novels chronicling the adventures of Lanny Budd, a fictional secret agent who participates in the major events of the twentieth century. *Dragon's Teeth*, an installment pitting Budd against Nazi Germany, earned Sinclair a Pulitzer Prize in 1943. But Sinclair's style of muckraking quickly fell out of fashion after World War II, as did the Socialist ideas he once held dear, and Sinclair's reputation declined. By the time he died in 1968, the ninety-year-old writer was judged according to new literary standards and considered a second-rate novelist by many literary critics.

Nevertheless, Upton Sinclair exerted a greater direct influence on American society than almost any other novelist of the twentieth century. Through his exposés of industrial and political corruption, beginning with *The Jungle,* he changed the nation in many practical ways during his long and exceptionally productive career.

Sinclair Lewis

Satirist of Middle-Class American Life
1885–1951

With the expansion of American industry and agriculture in the early twentieth century, many factory and farm towns in the Midwest grew at a rapid rate and earned a new national influence. With this influence came a new confidence, a sense of cultural and moral superiority that some observers found false, restrictive, and stifling. Chief among these observers was Sinclair Lewis, a brilliant satirist who emerged from the very region he ridiculed in his celebrated novels to change the way Americans saw themselves.

Harry Sinclair Lewis was born on February 7, 1885, in Sauk Centre, Minnesota, a prairie town of three thousand people. Awkward in appearance and bored with what he considered the narrow lifestyle of Sauk Centre, Lewis retreated into literature, as both an omnivorous reader and a prolific writer. He eventually escaped his hometown by enrolling at Yale University in Connecticut, where he wrote for the school literary magazine and began publishing his work in popular magazines. During his college years, he also embarked on several journeys through the United States, Central America, and Europe, and even worked in a commune run by muckraking novelist Upton Sinclair, all in an attempt to compensate for the monotony of his childhood. Graduating in 1907, he lived in several American cities, worked for a variety of publications, and published four novels and a play before writing his first work of merit, *Main Street* (1920).

The story of Carol Kennicott, a college-educated woman who finds herself trapped in a passionless marriage and living in a dull, unsophisticated town modeled after Lewis's own Sauk Centre, *Main Street* was the first of Lewis's critical, satirical novels about middle-class American life. A scathing assault on mainstream American culture, it created an immediate sensation in the United

> She wanted to run, fleeing from the encroaching prairie, demanding the security of a great city. Her dreams of creating a beautiful town were ludicrous. Oozing out from every drab wall, she felt a forbidding spirit which she could never conquer.
>
> ∼ From *Main Street*

States and was an instant bestseller. In 1922, Lewis expanded and refined his critique with *Babbitt*, a portrait of a small-minded midwestern businessman. The book was so popular and influential that its title became a common word in American society; anyone who narrowly pursued business interests over cultural or spiritual pursuits became known as a Babbitt.

Inspired by these early successes, Lewis in 1925 published *Arrowsmith*, a novel about scientific and intellectual mediocrity in the American heartland. *Arrowsmith* won the 1926 Pulitzer Prize, but Lewis rejected the award to maintain his position as a dangerous social critic. He enhanced this outsider reputation with the publication of *Elmer Gantry*, his 1927 novel depicting an evangelical preacher who preys on desperate church-goers, and *Dodsworth* (1929), about an automobile manufacturer living an unfulfilling emotional life. In each of these novels, Lewis's main concern was the American obsession with "respectability," and the cultural and intellectual limitations that Americans placed upon one another to maintain respectable appearances.

Many of Lewis's best novels, including *Arrowsmith* and *Elmer Gantry*, were later adapted for Hollywood; the movie versions reinforced Lewis's public image as an insightful critic of Middle America. But his private life was more complicated, and more tragic, than his books. By the mid-1920s, Lewis was suffering the effects of alcoholism. In addition, his unsettled, nomadic lifestyle took its toll on his health and his writing. So when he became in 1930 the first American to win the Nobel Prize for literature, his best work was already behind him. Though he continued to write harsh, satirical novels about a wide range of topics—including American race relations, corruption at academic institutions, fraud in the social services, and the dangers of political opportunism in America—Lewis failed to recapture his earlier bite and popularity. And despite being one of the literary world's premier observers of American culture, he spent the last years of his life in Europe, nursing a series of alcohol-related illnesses. He died in Rome in 1951, having published twenty-two novels and three plays.

Lewis's reputation diminished in the later years of his career. He had risen to prominence during a revolution in world literature, but he did not participate in the changes. As he was publishing his greatest satires in the 1920s, modernist writers such as F. Scott Fitzgerald, William Faulkner, and Ernest Hemingway were producing sophisticated, difficult, experimental works that made Lewis's novels appear simplistic. His style of writing soon fell out of fashion, but his books never entirely lost their hold on the American consciousness. Because of Lewis's critiques, Americans became more skeptical of their Main Streets, less complimentary about their Babbitts, and more likely to question the assumptions of ordinary, middle-class American life than before.

Ezra Pound

Controversial Poet, Literary Innovator
1885–1972

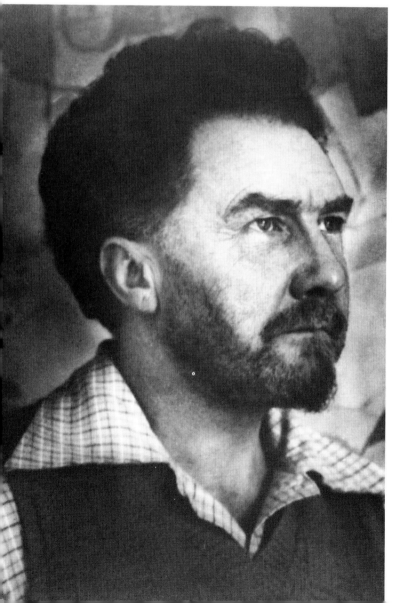

In his all-consuming devotion to poetry, Ezra Pound was extraordinary even among the other great writers of the early twentieth century. Few shared his knowledge of literary history, his determination to revive poetry in the modern world, or his skill as an artist. Even fewer could combine all of these elements in their work. But the single-mindedness that made Pound a great poet also has a less positive influence on his life. While he may have been the most generous literary adviser of his era, he was also capable of shocking cruelty, and his literary legacy is complicated by his personal and political failings.

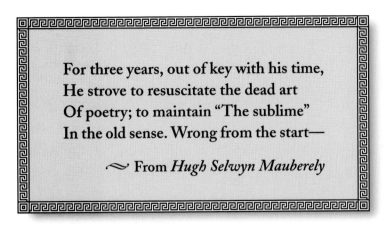

For three years, out of key with his time,
He strove to resuscitate the dead art
Of poetry; to maintain "The sublime"
In the old sense. Wrong from the start—

~ From *Hugh Selwyn Mauberely*

Pound was born in Hailey, Idaho, and grew up in Wyncote, a neighborhood of Philadelphia, Pennsylvania. At an early age, he decided to pursue a career as a poet. This ambition determined the course he would follow for the rest of his life. He graduated from Hamilton College in 1905, having transferred from the University of Pennsylvania two years earlier, then returned to the University of Pennsylvania the following year to study romance languages and Renaissance literature. Steeped in the history of poetry, he took a teaching job at Wabash College in Indiana and devoted more of his time to writing. But Pound felt confined while living in the Midwest and searched for a more comfortable atmosphere for poets. He left America, traveled through Europe, and in 1908 settled in London, where he worked as a secretary for the celebrated Irish poet William Butler Yeats.

In addition to serving Yeats, Pound wrote several volumes of poetry during his first years in Europe and worked as an agent for several American and European literary magazines. In this capacity, he discovered and encouraged many of the twentieth century's greatest writers, including American poets T. S. Eliot and Robert Frost, American novelist Ernest Hemingway, and Irish novelist James Joyce. With his friendship, support, and editorial assistance, these and many other expatriate writers found their distinct literary voices as well as new audiences for their work.

Pound also perfected his own poetic style in the early decades of the century. Like his friend Eliot, Pound came to see poetry as the most appropriate medium for criticizing modern life, and he wrote increasingly complex poems to mirror the increasing complexity of the world around him. Drawing on the history of Western poetry as well as a variety of religions, philosophies, economic theories, and languages—some of his poems even include Chinese characters—Pound wrote poems that were too difficult to be popular. However, an important group of artists, writers, and scholars discovered new techniques in Pound's writing, and he provided the foundation for the literary schools of imagism (based on visual images), vorticism (based on ideas of motion), and, ultimately, modernism, which encompassed most artistic experimentation in the first half of the twentieth century. Among his best work was the 1920 satire *Hugh Selwyn Mauberley*, which described his disenchantment with American culture, and *The Cantos*, a sprawling epic he began in 1917 and left incomplete at the time of his death in 1972.

The Cantos was Pound's crowning achievement, a series of 116 challenging poems describing the failures of Western history and the evils of capitalism. Unfortunately, it also revealed Pound's ethnic prejudices, including his anti-Semitism, and anticipated his greatest failures. In his quest for a receptive audience for his poems, Pound moved to Italy in 1925. The Italian dictator, Benito Mussolini, praised Pound's work. In return, Pound supported Mussolini's government and recorded radio broadcasts defending his policies, even after Mussolini aligned himself with Adolf Hitler during World War II. When the Allies defeated Italy in 1945, Pound was arrested as a war criminal and taken to Washington, D.C., to be tried for treason. Before the trial, however, Pound was declared legally insane and sent to a hospital, where he remained until Hemingway, Frost, Eliot, and other writers lobbied for his release in 1958. Afterward, Pound returned to Italy and lived there, writing but not publishing, until his death.

Pound's legacy is a troubled one. His literary innovations and the invaluable guidance he provided to some of the greatest writers of his era place him among the most important literary figures of the twentieth century. But his politics and his support of the Fascist campaigns in Europe suggest that he was also politically misguided, bigoted, and even dangerous. Critics have yet to decide whether the poetry or the politics are more important to the evaluation of his life and work.

T. S. Eliot

Modernist Poet, Critic
1888–1965

In some ways, Thomas Stearns Eliot was an unlikely figure to steer one of the most profound changes in modern writing. He was born in St. Louis, Missouri in 1888, far from the cultural capitals of America and Europe, and far from the cosmopolitan culture that would inspire the modernist literary movement he would help to found.

Nevertheless, his father, a prosperous businessman with family roots in New England, sent Eliot to the finest schools on the East Coast—Milton Academy and Harvard University—where he quickly displayed his intellectual gifts. At Harvard, Eliot studied philosophy and by 1910 earned a master's degree under the guidance of George

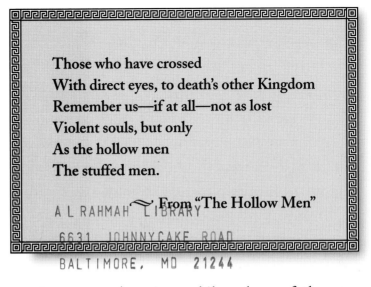

Those who have crossed
With direct eyes, to death's other Kingdom
Remember us—if at all—not as lost
Violent souls, but only
As the hollow men
The stuffed men.

From "The Hollow Men"

Santayana, one of the most important American philosophers of the era. Restless and ambitious for literary fame, Eliot then studied linguistics, poetry, and philosophy at the Sorbonne in Paris and at Oxford University in England. The older cultural and social practices of England appealed to Eliot, and he settled there after he completed his studies, working as a banker and writing poetry.

In 1917 he published his first volume, *Prufrock and Other Observations*. The title poem, "The Love Song of J. Alfred Prufrock," was Eliot's first masterpiece, a monologue spoken by an indecisive man confronting an increasingly complicated, intimidating, and wasteful world. Several other volumes followed, all exploring the same themes of intellectual and spiritual confusion, culminating in a long poem that had a tremendous impact on Western literature: *The Waste Land* (1922). A sprawling and episodic poem comparing the modern world to a trash heap, it gave voice to the pessimism and discouragement felt by many writers and artists after World War I. But *The Waste Land* was even more important for its stylistic innovations. Originally a loose collection of poetic scenes, Eliot and fellow American poet Ezra Pound edited the poem to make it less an expression of Eliot's life, less like the rhyming poems of the Victorian era, and more like a scholarly work, incorporating images from Eastern religion as well as from Western popular culture. The poem's complex and impersonal tone soon became a model for other poets of Eliot's era and a key characteristic of later modernist writings.

On the success of "Prufrock" and *The Waste Land*, Eliot based an expanding and varied literary career: He founded a literary journal called *The Criterion* in 1922; he joined a publishing company, Faber and Faber, in 1925; and he became an influential critic and teacher, producing such influential analyses as 1933's *The Use of Poetry and the Use of Criticism*, based on a lecture series he delivered at Harvard. He also continued to write poems, some of which, like "The Hollow Men" (1925), revisited the themes of *The Waste Land*. But after becoming a British citizen and a member of the Anglican Church in 1927—a culmination of his lifelong infatuation with English culture—Eliot shifted his focus from cultural to spiritual matters, and his work became less bleak.

His 1935 play, *Murder in the Cathedral*, recounted the story of Archbishop Thomas à Becket, a Catholic saint who had opposed the power of the king of England and been assassinated in 1170. Similarly, Eliot's last major poetic work, the poem cycle *Four Quartets* (1943), explored the philosophical and intellectual bases of the Christian faith. Even his late comic plays, including *The Cocktail Party* (1949), imported religious themes to the popular stage. Of course, none of Eliot's stage creations would be as popular or as financially successful as the stage musical *Cats*. Andrew Lloyd Webber's 1981 adaptation of Eliot's 1939 children's book, *Old Possum's Book of Practical Cats*, became one of the longest-running shows in Broadway history.

As a poet of enormous skill, a critic of remarkable range and influence, and an innovator at the vanguard of the modernist movement in world literature, T. S. Eliot emerged as one of the most important literary figures of the twentieth century. For his achievements, he was awarded the Nobel Prize for literature in 1948. An American-born writer, he was recognized as a giant in world literature at the time of his death in 1965.

Eugene O'Neill

Nobel Prize–Winning Playwright
1888–1953

When Eugene O'Neill began writing plays, American drama was based on old-fashioned conventions. Idealized characters and melodramatic plotlines dominated the popular stage. But over the course of a forty-year career, O'Neill transformed the theater. By combining a more realistic, psychological approach to his characters with a willingness to experiment, he created plays that were both profound and sensitive to the lives and dreams of individuals.

O'Neill was steeped in the history of theater at an early age. His father, James O'Neill, was a popular actor of the late nineteenth century, an Irish immigrant famous for playing the title role in the stage version of *The Count of Monte Cristo.* He and his wife frequently traveled to different cities with his acting troupe, and Eugene was born in a hotel in New York's theater district. Though his mother disliked the theater and the wandering lifestyle of its actors, O'Neill joined his father on the road and acted in some productions as a child. The only stability he knew during his early years he found at his family's summer home in New London, Connecticut; his boarding school; and finally as a student at Princeton University. But by the time he entered college, he was already displaying signs of the alcoholism which would plague him for the rest of his life, and was expelled for bad behavior before graduating.

For the next several years, he experimented with a variety of jobs and lifestyles. He was a seaman, a gold prospector in South America, a newspaper reporter in New London, and an actor and manager with his father's acting troupe. But it was not until 1912, when he was recovering from a bout of tuberculosis and reading the classics of dramatic history, that he decided on a career as a playwright. In 1914 he attended a Harvard theatrical workshop, which prepared him for his 1915 debut as a playwright with an experimental theater group in Provincetown, Massachusetts.

> I was born condemned to be one of those who has to see all sides of a question. When you're damned like that, the questions multiply for you until in the end it's all question and no answer.
>
> ∼ From *The Iceman Cometh*

His first plays were short, rich in realistic detail and dialogue, and based on his experiences at sea. To an American public accustomed to classically staged dramas and comedies about the behavior of the middle and upper classes, O'Neill's intensely psychological plots and characterizations represented a radical shift. Though such experimentation was often met with public hostility, his innovations were quickly rewarded by both audiences and critics. In 1920 he won the Pulitzer Prize for *Beyond the Horizon,* his first full-length play and his first Broadway production. During the same year, he staged *The Emperor Jones,* one of the first major American dramas to feature African American actors. During the next ten years, he produced several classics of American theater: *The Hairy Ape* (1922), a surrealist exploration of human aggression; *All God's Chillun Got Wings* (1924), an account of a racially mixed marriage; *Desire Under the Elms* (1924), importing ideas from Greek tragedy to a New England farm setting; and *Mourning Becomes Electra* (1931), another Greek-inspired drama set against the background of the American Civil War. He also received three more Pulitzers.

After the 1933 production of his only comedy, the popular *Ah, Wilderness!,* O'Neill withdrew from the public for several years. Stricken with Parkinson's disease, a nervous disorder that weakened him physically and would eventually kill him, he continued to write and even improved upon his style and techniques. He accepted the 1936 Nobel Prize for literature, the first American playwright to be so honored, and then set to work on his late masterpieces. When he emerged from relative silence with the 1946 production of *The Iceman Cometh,* he was crafting some of his most personal and best works.

With *The Iceman Cometh,* a tragedy about the lonely patrons of a saloon and the traveling salesman who inspires their dreams, O'Neill began to explore the circumstances of his past. He continued to mine this past in a series of plays that were written during the 1940s but produced during the 1950s, including *A Moon for the Misbegotten* (1943) and his masterpiece, *Long Day's Journey into Night*. Written between 1939 and 1941—but staged in 1956, three years after O'Neill's death—*Long Day's Journey into Night* was his most autobiographical play. In it, he examined the relationships and regrets of a family much like his own: an aging stage actor, his dissatisfied wife, and their two sons—one an alcoholic, the other a sailor. It won the 1957 Pulitzer Prize, the first ever awarded to an author after his death.

O'Neill incorporated unusual stage directions and settings in plays that were otherwise noteworthy for their realistic portrayals of human interactions. In this way, he managed to create dramas that were intensely personal as well as symbolic of universal human themes. His typical characters were seldom heroes in the classical sense. Instead, they were dreamers who struggled with their own weaknesses. And they captured the new realities of American life in the twentieth century. By the time he died in 1953, O'Neill had amassed an impressively varied body of work, ushered in a new kind of drama, and inspired a new generation of playwrights, including Tennessee Williams and Arthur Miller, whose works would put American plays at the center of world drama.

Zora Neale Hurston

Harlem Renaissance Writer of Fiction and Folklore
1891–1960

American readers rediscovered the writings of Zora Neale Hurston in the 1970s. During that decade, African Americans were continuing to build on the achievements of the Civil Rights struggle, pressing for social and political equality, and women were revitalizing the feminist movement. Though written a half-century earlier, Hurston's work—which expressed her devotion to

African American culture as well as her desire for racial and sexual equality—was a vital and important combination of these two political impulses.

Until the 1970s, however, Hurston was a forgotten figure. She had died, penniless, in 1960. One of the most remarkable women in American literature, she was a victim of both racism and sexism and spent the final decade of her life working as a newspaper reporter, a substitute teacher, a librarian, and finally a cleaning woman.

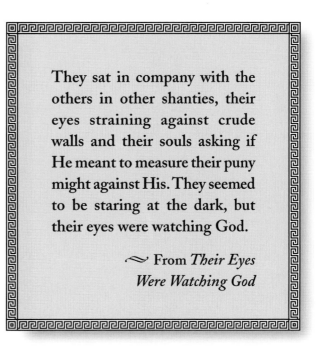

They sat in company with the others in other shanties, their eyes straining against crude walls and their souls asking if He meant to measure their puny might against His. They seemed to be staring at the dark, but their eyes were watching God.

~ From *Their Eyes Were Watching God*

Hurston was born in the all-black town of Eatonville, Florida, in 1891. Despite an unsettled childhood, during which she cared for her brother's children, joined a theater group as a wardrobe girl, and worked as a maid, she gained admittance to Howard University and then to Barnard College and Columbia University, where she studied anthropology. Her research focused on collections of African American folklore. Hurston was particularly interested in the ways in which people from rural communities adapted the English language into specialized dialects. She published the myths and stories she discovered during her research excursions in her 1935 collection, *Mules and Men,* and used them as source material for some of her best fiction. Later she would collect folklore from Jamaica, Haiti, Bermuda, and Honduras as well, publishing several of her discoveries in 1938's *Tell My Horse.*

In the 1920s and early 1930s, Columbia University and the surrounding Harlem community became the center of the Harlem Renaissance, a period of intense experimentation in African American literature, music, and the visual arts. Hurston became a prominent participant in this vibrant movement. Like Langston Hughes, a young writer of the period with whom she edited a literary magazine in 1926, Hurston began publishing short stories in the major literary journals of the day. Some of her stories, like "Spunk" (1925), were based on the myths she recorded during her journeys through the South. Others, like "Muttsy" (1926), explored African American life in the inner city. Still others, like "The Gilded Six-Bits" (1933), addressed the plight of women in a world dominated by men.

These stories, startlingly original in their own right, prepared Hurston to write her best novels, *Jonah's Gourd Vine* (1934) and *Their Eyes Were Watching God* (1937). Chronicling the life of Janie Crawford, a Southern black woman who survives three marriages and struggles to understand her place in a racially segregated, male-dominated society, *Their Eyes Were Watching God* combined Hurston's interests in African American folklore and dialect with a unique, evocative prose style. It is now considered one of the finest American novels of the twentieth century, but Hurston's peers had already begun to reject her work by the time it was published.

In the late 1930s and the 1940s, many African American writers called for literature with a clear political agenda, such as Richard Wright's novel *Native Son,* which explicitly attacked mainstream American society. In contrast, Hurston's fiction addressed race relations more subtly, often through the lens of women's issues, and in ways that emphasized the day-to-day lives of its characters rather than their political involvements. As African American writers such as Wright produced angrier, more graphic novels, Hurston was brushed aside. Even though she had overcome tremendous obstacles—as a poor, Southern black woman who had conquered the New York literary scene—she could not regain her position in the new political climate. To survive, she held a variety of jobs in her later years, each more distant from the literary community than the last. Suffering a stroke in October 1959 and dying early the next year, she did not leave enough money behind for a tombstone.

It would take a very different political climate and a very different group of readers—including Hurston's most influential champion, novelist Alice Walker—to secure her rightful place in American literary history. Hurston herself never saw the restoration of her literary reputation. But her fiction, which explored the political and social conflicts within the African American community while preserving the dialects and traditions of an evolving black culture, has survived as a rich mine for scholars and a treasure for readers.

Jean Toomer

African American Writer Best Known for Cane
1894–1967

*J*ean Toomer lived on both sides of the twentieth-century color line, in both white and black communities. That was one of the things that made him a unique writer. But it was also a difficult way to live in the era before the Civil Rights movement. Few writers depicted the conflicts between white and black Americans in the twentieth century as artistically as Toomer did in his collection, *Cane.* Even fewer felt as personally divided by those conflicts or sacrificed as much to overcome them.

Toomer was born on December 26, 1894, the son of parents with mixed racial backgrounds. His grandfather, the man who raised him, was the first black governor of Louisiana, P. B. S. Pinchback. Growing up in the Pinchback home, situated in a diverse community in Washington, D.C., Toomer was shielded from racial conflict. Then, when he was fourteen, he moved into an uncle's home in an African American section of the city. There he adopted the strategy he would adhere to for the rest of his life: He claimed to be a new kind of American, neither black nor white, and took no sides.

Immediately after high school, he attended the University of Wisconsin, where he studied agriculture for a single term. For the next several years, he transferred from one college to another in search of a course of study and a career that interested him. By 1916 he changed direction entirely, abandoning his education for a newfound interest in radical politics. He began offering political lectures on a variety of topics, including socialism and women's rights, and continued to lecture through World War I. At the same time, he worked as a teacher and a car salesman, studied music, and most important, began writing fiction. All of this activity taxed him physically and emotionally, and he was

> Up from the skeleton stone walls, up from the rotting floor boards and the solid hand-hewn beams of oak of the pre-war cotton factory, dusk came. Up from the dusk the full moon came.... The full moon in the great door was an omen. Negro women improvised songs against its spell.
>
> ~ From *Cane*

soon forced to choose a single career path. In 1920 he decided to focus almost exclusively on his writing.

He published little at first, but he studied closely the works of his contemporaries—including the modernist writers who were experimenting with new literary forms—and honed his own techniques. During the summer of 1921, in order to support himself as an unpublished writer, he took a job at a technical school for African Americans in Sparta, Georgia. There he discovered the subject matter and the literary voice that he would perfect in his masterpiece: *Cane*.

Cane is an unusual book, a collection of short stories, sketches, and poems that blend together to create something like a novel. The first half of the book is devoted to the lives of African American men and women in the rural South, people surviving economic hardships and social frustrations. The second half traces the effects of racism in American cities. As a whole, the book addresses the questions of racial identity and social division that Toomer struggled with throughout his life. And it does so through a musical, haunting writing style that sets it apart from most other works of its time, one that turns scenes of violence and oppression into poetry.

Cane appeared in 1923, early in the period of intense African American creativity known as the Harlem Renaissance. It influenced many of the younger black writers of the era and set a high standard for the literature coming out of New York City in the 1920s. But Toomer's personal influence began to wane almost as soon as the book was published. First, he rejected the notion that he was an African American writer; despite his Pinchback heritage, he wished to be known simply as an American. This made him an unusual figure at a time when the writers and artists of the Harlem Renaissance were celebrating African American achievements. Even more surprising, instead of following up his acclaimed debut with more of his poetic fiction, he discarded his artistic theories almost entirely. In 1923 he became a spokesman for several self-help techniques then gaining popularity. Thereafter, he wrote novels, essays, and poems based on his ideas about self-improvement. He sold little of this new work, which did not satisfy readers or critics who remembered the beauty of his first efforts, and withdrew from mainstream American culture. He even had to pay a printer to publish the only book he released after *Cane.*

Toomer was largely forgotten by the time he died in 1967, more than thirty years after writing the book that earned him a place among the masters of twentieth-century fiction. Unable to resolve questions about his own racial identity, he spent most of his life searching for a new identity. And his search ultimately took him out of the limelight. Still, in 1923 he poured all of his doubts and concerns into the poems and stories of *Cane* and produced one of the most beautiful works of the Harlem Renaissance.

John Dos Passos

Author of Sweeping Social and Political Novels
1896–1970

The world was a very different place for American writers after World War I. Convinced that modern warfare, modern industry, and the conveniences of modern life demanded a new kind of literature, most sought new forms of expression. Yet even among these experimental writers, John Dos Passos was unique. By dedicating both his literature and his life to the exploration and analysis of the modern world, he proved to be one of the most expansive and searching literary figures of the twentieth century.

Born in 1896 in Chicago, Dos Passos spent much of his early childhood traveling the United States and Europe with his mother. Equally uncomfortable on both continents, he was shy, unpopular, and withdrawn, particularly during his years at Choate School in Connecticut and Harvard University. The bookish Dos Passos found his purpose in life after graduation, and in a most unexpected place, when he returned to war-torn Europe. Originally visiting Spain to study architecture, he soon found himself a participant in World War I. Like his future friend Ernest Hemingway, he became an ambulance driver for the French army, for the Red Cross, and finally for the U.S. Army medical corps. Following these years of service, he stayed in Europe as a war correspondent for American newspapers.

> There are flags on all the flagpoles up Fifth Avenue. In the shrill wind of history the great flags flap and tug at their lashings on the creaking goldknobbed poles up Fifth Avenue. The stars jiggle sedately against the slate sky, the red and white stripes writhe against the clouds.
>
> ∼ From *Manhattan Transfer*

The war soured his impressions of the modern world. After witnessing the unprecedented destruction in Europe, he began work on two antiwar novels, *One Man's Initiation: 1917* (1920) and the acclaimed *Three Soldiers* (1921). In these novels he began to explore the radical political ideas for which he would be known through the next two decades. A defender of workers' and immigrants' rights, Dos Passos became an outspoken critic of American society in his writing as well as in his public life. For a time, he was also a leading advocate of American socialism.

Concerned with social justice and human rights, he stretched the boundaries of his fiction to include a wide variety of peoples and a wide array of political and social scenarios. His first major work, 1925's *Manhattan Transfer*, portrayed life in New York City from nearly every perspective—poor and wealthy, male and female, immigrant and native. It also introduced the experimental features for which Dos Passos would be most famous: the "newsreel" technique of including quotes from newspapers, advertisements, and popular songs, and the "camera eye" technique that incorporated the writer's own voice into the novel.

Armed with these methods, Dos Passos spent the next ten years completing an even more ambitious work, a trilogy of novels—*The 42nd Parallel* (1930), *1919* (1932), and *The Big Money* (1936)—covering the full range of the American experience. The trilogy, which he called *U. S. A.*, was an enormous undertaking and placed him among the very best and most important American writers of the age, which included his close friends Hemingway and F. Scott Fitzgerald.

But as his political philosophy began to change in the late 1930s, his fiction changed as well. Having witnessed the Spanish Civil War firsthand in the 1930s as well as the early skirmishes of World War II, Dos Passos recognized that several of his beliefs, including socialism, were now held by America's enemies. Slowly he shed these beliefs and at the same time abandoned many of his experimental literary techniques. His later work, with the exception of 1961's *Midcentury*, was more conservative both politically and stylistically, and less successful than his novels of the 1920s and 1930s.

In later years, he feverishly produced volumes of fiction, essays, and even biography, and although he never regained his place of prominence as a fiction writer, he remained a well-regarded critic and intellectual through the later half of the twentieth century. A writer noteworthy for his limitless imagination as well as for his ground-breaking experiments, Dos Passos continued to explore the political complexities of the modern world, and of American society in particular, until his death in 1970.

F. Scott Fitzgerald

Jazz-Age Novelist, Short-Story Writer
1896–1940

World War I ended in 1919, and the stock market crashed in 1929. During the decade in between, the United States experienced one of the most extraordinary economic booms in its history. Many Americans enjoyed a seemingly limitless prosperity, spending extravagantly on homes, cars, and entertainment. The writer who gave this period its nickname—the Jazz Age—and many of its most lasting images was F. Scott Fitzgerald.

Fitzgerald was born on September 24, 1896, in St. Paul, Minnesota. His mother's family had once been prominent in the St. Paul community but had fallen on difficult economic times. Named after a famous ancestor, Francis Scott Key, who wrote "The Star Spangled Banner," Fitzgerald spent his whole life trying to regain the status his family lost. He attended several elite prep schools, where he proved to be an indifferent student. But in 1913, despite his mediocre grades, he was accepted at Princeton University, thus fulfilling a childhood dream. Still neglecting his schoolwork, he devoted most of his time to literary and theatrical organizations and left Princeton without graduating in 1917. In that year, Fitzgerald received his commission from the army and prepared to take part in World War I. The war ended before the eager Fitzgerald reached the battlefront, but his war experience was not a total disappointment to him. In 1918, while stationed at a base in Montgomery, Alabama, he met Zelda Sayre, a beautiful, free-spirited debutante who became the love of his life.

He moved to New York City after the war, where he hoped to begin a career as a fiction writer. His work paid off in 1920, when he published *This Side of Paradise,* his first novel. The story of a Princeton student's first attempts at love

> They got in their automobiles which bore them out to Long Island, and somehow they ended up at Gatsby's door. . . . Sometimes they came and went without having met Gatsby at all, came for the party with a simplicity of heart that was its own ticket of admission.
>
> ～ From *The Great Gatsby*

and fame, it skillfully portrayed the youthful, vibrant culture of postwar America and became a best-seller. He and Zelda, whom he married later in the year, became instant celebrities, the nation's favorite couple. Attractive, eloquent, and carefree, they seemed to perfectly represent the spirit of the Jazz Age. They spent whatever money they had on expensive dinners, late-night parties, and other luxuries. Theirs was a troubled marriage, however. Fitzgerald drank too much, and Zelda suffered from schizophrenia, a disease that would plague her for the next twenty years.

After publishing several collections of short stories and another novel, *The Beautiful and Damned* (1922), Fitzgerald followed many other American writers—including his friends Gertrude Stein and Ernest Hemingway—and moved to Paris in 1924. There he began the novel that would seal his reputation, *The Great Gatsby*. Published in 1925, *Gatsby* is the story of a wealthy and mysterious Midwesterner who throws elaborate parties at his Long Island mansion to attract the attention of the woman he loves. Though it celebrates the glamour of wealth in the 1920s, its tragic conclusion serves as a warning to a nation living wastefully and foolishly. More impressive than the plot, however, is the vibrant, graceful style in which the novel is written. At his best, in novels like *The Great Gatsby* and in a handful of short stories, Fitzgerald wrote musically and directly, adapting the richness of poetry to his prose. Despite its enormous strengths, however, *Gatsby* did not attract a wide readership when it was first published. It sold poorly throughout Fitzgerald's lifetime but has since become recognized as one of the finest American novels ever written.

Following the commercial failure of *The Great Gatsby*, Fitzgerald's alcoholism and Zelda's mental illness began to take a serious toll on his life and work. He enjoyed fewer successes in the following years and experienced long periods during which he was unable to write at all. He managed a handful of acclaimed short stories, including "Babylon Revisited" and "Crazy Sunday," which suggested that he had not lost his ability entirely. And in 1934 he published *Tender Is the Night,* a fictionalized account of his troubled marriage that briefly restored his reputation as a leading American novelist. But he could not recapture the brilliance of *Gatsby.* He seemed to lose control of his stories as well as of his drinking in the 1930s and 1940s. Deep in debt and desperate for money, he tried his hand at Hollywood screenplays as well as a series of minor stories for American magazines. He remained a popular story writer, but his self-destructive behavior discouraged others from working with him. And Zelda's psychological breakdown, which forced her to live the remainder of her life in psychiatric institutions, proved too painful for him to bear.

On December 21, 1940, forty-four-year-old Fitzgerald died of a massive heart attack, likely stemming from his alcoholism. Among the writings he left behind was an unfinished manuscript later published as *The Last Tycoon,* one of his best novels. The story of a Hollywood producer who, like Fitzgerald himself, lived an important and romantic life despite tragic consequences, *The Last Tycoon* might have revived Fitzgerald's career, had he lived to finish it. Unfinished, it nevertheless remains a beautiful piece of writing, a prime example of Fitzgerald's elegant style, and a fitting end to a brilliant and troubled life.

William Faulkner

Novelist of Southern Life and History
1897–1962

Of the major writers of the World War I generation—which included Ernest Hemingway and F. Scott Fitzgerald—William Faulkner experienced the slowest rise to fame. Initially readers were intimidated by his difficult, complex novels about the American South. By the mid-1940s, most of his works were out of print. But Faulkner witnessed a surge of interest in his work before he died in

1962, and he is now considered among the giants of twentieth-century world literature.

William Faulkner was born on September 25, 1897, in New Albany, Mississippi, and grew up in nearby Oxford. Like many of the families he would describe in his novels, his family had lived in Mississippi for generations. His great-grandfather had been a planter, a Civil War officer, a railroad magnate, and even the author of a popular novel. But by the time he was born, the Falkners (the novelist would later add a "u" to his name) were less influential in Mississippi society.

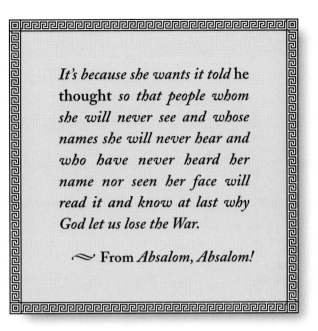

It's because she wants it told he thought *so that people whom she will never see and whose names she will never hear and who have never heard her name nor seen her face will read it and know at last why God let us lose the War.*

～ From *Absalom, Absalom!*

Faulkner dropped out of high school in 1915 and worked in his family's bank in Oxford, Mississippi. When the United States entered World War I in 1917, he tried to enlist in the army. Too short (at five feet, six inches) to satisfy army requirements, he then tried to enlist in the Canadian Royal Flying Corps. After lying about his age and birthplace and claiming to be a British citizen, he was accepted. The war ended before he completed his training, but Faulkner returned to Oxford in 1919 wearing an officer's uniform that he had purchased and lying about his experiences in combat.

He enrolled at the University of Mississippi after the war, even though he never received a high-school diploma. While a student, he published several poems in local and national publications. Encouraged by these early successes, he left the university after three semesters to earn his living as a writer. After moving to New Orleans to find work as a newspaper reporter, he met a group of fiction writers, including novelist Sherwood Anderson, who encouraged him to develop his fiction and poetry. He quickly published a volume of poems, *The Marble Faun* (1924), in a limited edition and drafted his first novel, *A Soldier's Pay,* which was published in 1926 to little notice.

In 1925 he moved to Paris and lived on the outskirts of the expatriate literary community that had gathered in the French capital. But unlike Hemingway and Fitzgerald, who also settled in Paris in the 1920s, Faulkner was too shy to prosper there. Within a few months of his arrival, he again returned to Oxford. This time he was determined to write about the community close at hand.

With *Sartoris,* the 1929 novel that introduced readers to the citizens of the fictional Yoknapatawpha County—based on his home county of Lafayette—Faulkner began to find his distinct voice as a novelist. His next novel, another installment of the Yoknapatawpha saga entitled *The Sound and the Fury* (1929), proved to be his first masterpiece. In its innovative narrative style, in which four characters tell separate versions of the same story, and in its psychologically rich portrait of a southern family in crisis, it represented a major advance in American writing. But *The Sound and the Fury,* like many of Faulkner's subsequent novels, proved too experimental for a wide audience at the time.

Later classics of the Yoknapatawpha sequence, including *As I Lay Dying* (1930), *Light in August* (1932), *Absalom, Absalom!* (1936), and *The Unvanquished* (1938), continued to feature disjointed narratives and an array of poetic techniques to express their characters' obsessions. They also dealt honestly with the conflicts at the heart of southern society, including the collapse of family traditions and the persistence of racial hatred in the late-nineteenth and early-twentieth centuries.

By returning to Yoknapatawpha intermittently throughout the rest of his career, Faulkner was able to dissect southern culture and create a mythology to rival any other in modern literature.

Despite his growing reputation in Europe—and the popularity of his gruesome 1931 novel *Sanctuary* and his 1939 novel *The Wild Palms*—American audiences generally ignored Faulkner's work. He was therefore forced to supplement his income by writing Hollywood movie scripts. Among his most successful efforts were the screenplays for two movies starring Humphrey Bogart and Lauren Bacall: *To Have and Have Not* (1945), based on a Hemingway novel, and *The Big Sleep* (1946), based on a novel by Raymond Chandler. He also wrote short stories for magazines and journals, including his most popular tales, "A Rose for Emily" and "The Bear." But Faulkner's novels were his chief interest, and he continued to write them at a frantic pace. Apparently the only obstacles to his creativity were his occasional battles with alcoholism. Nevertheless, most of his novels were out of print by the mid-1940s.

With the 1946 publication of *The Portable Faulkner*, a compilation aimed at readers of popular fiction, he finally began to reach new audiences. And when he was awarded the 1949 Nobel Prize for literature, based on the strength of his reputation in Europe, he finally achieved a measure of prestige at home. Two of his later novels, *A Fable* (1954) and *The Reivers* (1962), even won Pulitzer Prizes. After laboring in relative obscurity for over twenty years, Faulkner became a prominent public figure. He participated in government writing programs, attended awards banquets, and even became a vocal supporter of the desegregation of southern institutions, though he opposed many of the immediate changes proposed by Civil Rights activists. His reputation had improved so dramatically that when he died in 1962, every major news outlet in America reported on his funeral.

Despite the accolades he received after winning the Nobel Prize, William Faulkner was never as popular as some of his literary peers. Less accessible than Hemingway and less glamorous than Fitzgerald, he did not appeal to American popular culture. Instead he was an artist who had the courage to chart his own course, to write in an unprecedented style about a previously ignored region of the world. As a literary innovator and an interpreter of southern American culture, he had no equal.

Ernest Hemingway

Fiction Writer, Journalist, International Celebrity
1899–1961

On July 8, 1918, in the last few months of World War I, Ernest Hemingway was a nineteen-year-old ambulance driver working for the Red Cross. He was stationed at an Italian battlefront near the town of Schio. Though he could not enlist as a soldier because of an eye problem, Hemingway was right where he wanted to be: in the thick of the action, close enough to the fighting

> There were many words that you could not stand to hear and finally only the names of places had dignity. . . . Abstract words such as glory, honor, courage, or hallow were obscene beside the concrete names of villages, the numbers of roads, the names of rivers, the numbers of regiments and the dates.
>
> ～ From *A Farewell to Arms*

to experience the thrills of combat. That night, he was badly wounded when an enemy mortar shell exploded near his foxhole. In the months following the explosion, his wounds would heal at army hospitals. But he would relive the experience for the rest of his life. In fact, it would become the inspiration for his greatest fiction.

World War I changed the way American and European writers thought about the world. They became disenchanted with the political leaders who had started the war and distrusted most of the leaders who followed. When the war was over, they wrote about a changed world, one that was more violent and less civilized. And they wrote in a style different from that of their predecessors; they experimented more. Hemingway's friend Gertrude Stein, also a writer, would call them a "lost generation" because they seemed so changed by, and yet cut off from, the recent past. And Hemingway, who knew the horrors of modern war firsthand, would become the most famous voice of that "lost generation."

Born on July 21, 1899, Hemingway grew up in the comfortable middle-class community of Oak Park, Illinois, a suburb of Chicago. At an early age, he began sacrificing some of that comfort for adventure and the kinds of experiences he could turn into literature. Refusing to attend college, he moved to Kansas City in 1917 to become a newspaper reporter. Then, after his stint in the war, he worked for a Toronto newspaper, mastering his craft. He liked to write about crime and sport, and that was how he earned his pay. But writing fiction was his passion.

Following the advice of novelist Sherwood Anderson, Hemingway moved to Paris at the end of 1921. Because of its low cost of living and its long history as a city of the arts, Paris was at the time a haven for poor writers. Hemingway joined a literary community that included Stein, the American experimental poet Ezra Pound, and later, novelist F. Scott Fitzgerald. In this environment, he blossomed. In 1923 he published his first book, *Three Stories and Ten Poems,* and in 1924 he published a slim volume of connected short stories, *In Our Time,* that marked the true beginning of his literary rise. These books introduced the writers of Paris, and later the world, to Hemingway's uniquely spare writing style, with its pattern of short sentences, and his often-violent subject matter. And his emphasis on action and exotic locations attracted a wide readership. His first two novels, *The Sun Also Rises* (1926), about the American community in Paris, and *A Farewell to Arms* (1929), based on Hemingway's wartime experiences, became immediate best-sellers. These early successes made Hemingway an international celebrity. More important, his restrained, gritty writing style became the standard for literary writing in the first half of the twentieth century.

In later years Hemingway would bolster his reputation with several successful novels and short stories, including "The Snows of Kilimanjaro" (1936), *For Whom the Bell Tolls* (1940), and *The Old Man and the Sea* (1952), a novel about a courageous fisherman that earned Hemingway a Pulitzer Prize and received special mention when he won the 1954 Nobel Prize for literature. Many of these later works were also adapted into popular movies, increasing Hemingway's stature as a pop culture icon.

But his exciting personal life contributed to his fame as much as his writing did. His hunting safaris and fishing expeditions, his love for bullfighting, and his participation in several battles of the Spanish Civil War and World War II became the stuff of legend. So too did his fondness for alcohol and his tough-guy persona. He seemed to live the lifestyle he wrote about, one filled with danger and adventure. Americans who never read his fiction often read about his activities in popular newspapers and magazines.

By the late 1950s, however, Hemingway's reckless lifestyle had taken its toll on his health and his writing ability. He wrote several weaker books and novels in his later years. He alienated friends and family members with his quick temper and unpredictability. And he suffered several freak accidents, including two plane crashes in 1953 that left him with serious head and neck injuries. Increasingly isolated and unable to write, Hemingway sank into a deep depression for which he received radical treatment. The injuries, the depression, and the treatment left him a shell of the man who once captured the world's imagination.

Hemingway committed suicide on July 2, 1961. It was a tragic end to a forty-year career that produced some of the most beloved works of American literature, works that both captured the changing times and changed the way later generations of writers would write.

Vladimir Nabokov

Russian Émigré, Novelist, Scholar
1899–1977

onsidered an American writer because his greatest works explored American themes and were written in English, Vladimir Nabokov was born in St. Petersburg, Russia, in 1899. He lived in several European countries, and spent nineteen years in residence in the United States, making him one of the most cosmopolitan writers in American literary history. Drawing on this unique, international perspective,

> Lolita, light of my life, fire of my loins. My sin, my soul. Lo-lee-ta: the tip of the tongue taking a trip of three steps down the palate to tap, at three, on the teeth. Lo. Lee. Ta.
>
> ～ From *Lolita*

he created some of the most unusual and sophisticated works of the twentieth century.

Nabokov's father was an influential liberal politician and an opponent of the Communist Party who escaped to Germany during the Russian revolution of 1917. Young Vladimir was studying at Trinity College in Cambridge, England, when his father was killed at a political rally in Berlin in 1922. After graduating from Trinity in 1922, Nabokov moved back to his family in Berlin, where he struggled to support himself. He wrote fiction and essays intended for the growing population of Russians who were leaving their war-torn nation and settling in Western Europe. He also supplemented his income by offering English lessons and composing crossword puzzles for the local newspaper. In the mid-1930s he moved to France, where he began writing fiction full-time, experimenting in English, and preparing for his 1940 emigration to the United States.

Between 1941 and 1948, Nabokov worked as a professor of literature at Wellesley College in Massachusetts. Then he transferred to Cornell University in New York, where he lived until 1959. During his stay at Cornell, he became a U.S. citizen and completed his most famous fictional work about American society: *Lolita*. The story of a middle-aged European intellectual who falls in love with an underaged American girl and takes her on a cross-country spree, *Lolita* scandalized audiences when it was published in Europe in 1955. And it caused enormous controversy when it reached American shores three years later. Nabokov intended his novel as an experiment in literary style as well as a moral warning to readers of fiction. Beautiful writing like that found in *Lolita* could be dangerous, he suggested, because it could make readers forget the abuse, violence, and criminal activity at the center of the story. Indeed, many readers had assumed that he had written an unconventional love story. But many other readers simply condemned it as immoral.

Lolita became an important cultural phenomenon and the subject of several movies. It also made Nabokov's reputation as an American writer. He followed its success with several other difficult but equally distinguished novels, including *Pnin* (1957) and *Pale Fire* (1962), both of which parodied the academic world that Nabokov had come to dominate. A man of diverse interests, he also published biographies, critical essays, and memoirs including *Speak, Memory* (1966) and devoted considerable energy to the scientific study of butterflies, which occupied the time he spent away from his books. In 1960, he left American university life for good and moved to Switzerland, where he lived and wrote until his death in 1977.

As a writer, Nabokov adopted the English language and turned to the United States for inspiration relatively late in his career. Nevertheless, in a ten-year span beginning when he was over fifty years old, he produced several of the most beautifully written, most intellectually challenging novels of his adoptive country, and of world literature in general.

Langston Hughes

Jazz Poet of the Harlem Renaissance
1902–1967

During the Harlem Renaissance of the 1920s, African American writers and artists rediscovered and celebrated the rich traditions of black culture. Paramount among these rediscoveries was the history of African American music, from the slave spirituals and work songs of the early nineteenth century to the gospel, blues, and jazz of the early twentieth century. These musical

> And far into the night he crooned that tune.
> The stars went out and so did the moon.
> The singer stopped playing and went to bed.
> While the Weary Blues echoes through his head.
> He slept like a rock or a man that's dead.
>
> ~ From *The Weary Blues*

forms influenced almost all of the art produced in Harlem during the era. But few writers were as indebted to music as Langston Hughes. Though he was also a novelist, an essayist, a journalist, and a playwright, it was Hughes's music-inspired poetry that made him one of the most distinctive American poets.

Born in Joplin, Missouri, in 1902, Hughes spent his childhood traveling the Midwest with his mother and stepfather as they looked for work. Accustomed to life on the road, he refused to settle down even after he graduated from Central High School in Cleveland in 1920. Instead he moved to Mexico City to live with his father. He experienced less racial prejudice in the capital of Mexico and found time to work on poems such as "The Negro Speaks of Rivers," which was published in *The Crisis*—a leading journal of the Harlem Renaissance—in 1921. After a year in Mexico, however, he left his father on the condition that he would study engineering at Columbia University in New York. But Hughes stayed at Columbia only for one year before he withdrew and boarded a steamer bound for Africa.

Hughes's journeys led him to Paris, where he worked as a restaurant busboy, and then to Washington D.C., where he worked for a publisher. But he never stopped writing poetry. The work he published during his travels earned him a growing reputation in Harlem. In 1925, after winning a poetry contest in *The*

Crisis and impressing several important white writers, Hughes signed a contract with a major publishing company and submitted his first book, *The Weary Blues* (1926). The next year, as he was completing his college degree at Lincoln University in Pennsylvania, he published his second volume, *Fine Clothes to the Jew* (1927). These two collections announced the arrival of a major new voice in American poetry.

Hughes's poems described the harsh realities of African American life in the rhythms of jazz and the blues. They featured the rhyme schemes of popular music and the kinds of language Hughes heard on the streets of New York and in the fields of the rural South and Midwest. To the disappointment of some, they were often critical of black as well as white Americans. But criticism was not Hughes's primary concern. His poems celebrated the richness of African American culture, in a style entirely derived from that culture.

In 1930, after the publication of his first novel, *Not Without Laughter*, Hughes left Harlem to tour the South as a lecturer and reader. Two years later he accompanied several other black intellectuals on a tour of the Soviet Union. Despite the shortcomings of that nation's communist system, Hughes found some reasons to praise the USSR, especially for avoiding the kind of racial segregation that was still a feature of life in the United States. Such praise was dangerous to his career, however. In 1953, when the U.S. government was investigating Americans with ties to the Soviet Union, Hughes was forced to deny his more radical political beliefs in order to continue writing.

When he returned from the USSR, he published a collection of short stories, *The Ways of White Folks* (1934) and founded a theatrical group, the Harlem Suitcase Players, to stage his plays. Then he lent his talents to the American war effort during World War II. He wrote advertisements for government bonds and columns supporting the war effort in *The Chicago Defender*. In the

Defender articles, he adopted the voice of a fictional character, Jesse B. Semple (or "Simple"), who would later become the subject of some of his most popular books, including 1950's *Simple Speaks His Mind*. He also continued to work with theater groups and publish his distinctive poetry, including his ground-breaking 1951 poem cycle, *Montage of a Dream Deferred*.

Through the 1960s, Hughes wrote in a variety of genres, edited collections of African American literature, and nurtured the careers of a new generation of black writers. Occasionally criticized by Civil Rights activists for his non-confrontational political style as well as his rejection of communist beliefs during his 1953 testimony before Congress, he nevertheless remained an influential figure in African American culture until his death in 1967.

Hughes participated in many aspects of American culture in the mid-twentieth century. As a journalist, a playwright, a novelist, an editor, and a memoirist, he made important and lasting contributions to the literature of his era. But his legacy to future generations begins with his poetry, and its unique adaptation of popular music to the representation of African American experiences.

John Steinbeck

Writer Best Known for Depression-Era Fiction
1902–1968

John Steinbeck believed that good writers had a responsibility to be good citizens. As a novelist, short-story writer, and journalist, he believed he had an obligation to observe, comment on, and help improve American society. In his greatest works, including the 1937 novella *Of Mice and Men*, the 1939 novel *The Grapes of Wrath*, and the 1961 novel *The Winter of Our Discontent*, he participated in the most significant political and social debates of his age. In the process, he became not only one of the nation's most popular novelists of the twentieth century but also one of the most important.

Steinbeck was born on February 27, 1902, in Salinas, California, the central town in a large farming region. Awkward in appearance and uncomfortable in public,

> I'll be ever'where—wherever you look. Wherever they's a fight so hungry people can eat, I'll be there. . . . An' when our folks eat the stuff they raise an' live in the houses they build— why, I'll be there.
>
> ∼ From *The Grapes of Wrath*

Steinbeck spent much of his childhood reading fantasy novels and legends, such as the tales of King Arthur. In 1919 he entered Stanford University. He showed promise in literature classes and more than a passing interest in marine biology, but he never learned to enjoy his schoolwork. He preferred his summer jobs, working on the farms and in the food-processing plants around Salinas, to his studies. And he preferred fiction writing to everything else. Failing to earn a degree, he left Stanford for good in 1925. In the following years, he held a variety of jobs while he wrote his first novel, a pirate tale called *Cup of Gold*, which was published in 1929. That book, as well as his next two, failed to find an audience and received little critical notice. In fact, Steinbeck would not achieve a real literary success until the 1935 publication of *Tortilla Flat*, a comic novel about the poor workers who lived in the hills around Monterey, California. *Tortilla Flat* introduced readers to the men and women Steinbeck would depict more seriously in his greatest writing: the poor farmers who settled in California during the Great Depression.

The depression was one of the nation's greatest trials. For ten years following the stock-market crash of 1929, the U.S. economy staggered. Millions of American lost their jobs and lived in poverty. The southwestern farm regions were hit particularly hard. But Steinbeck found himself in a position to help them. First as a worker and later as a reporter, Steinbeck lived among the farmers who were too poor to own land during the 1930s and who were therefore forced to migrate from region to region looking for work. He turned their experiences into fiction. He wrote about a farm labor strike in *In Dubious Battle* (1936) and about workers who dreamed of a better life in *Of Mice and Men*. Then, in the mix of journalism and fiction that made up his greatest work, *The Grapes of Wrath*, he followed a migrant family from Oklahoma as it struggled to survive the long journey to California. All of these works called attention to the plight of migrant farmers and inspired other Americans to assist them. They also made Steinbeck a national celebrity, a friend to presidents such as Franklin Roosevelt and Lyndon Johnson, and a recognizable champion of the poor and underprivileged.

In subsequent writings, Steinbeck continued to address the most pressing issues of his time. He reported on American troops fighting in World War II and the Vietnam War. He visited the Soviet Union, the nation's primary opponent during the cold war, and chronicled the lifestyles of its citizens. And he observed the early Civil Rights movement, lending support to the African American struggle for equality. In some of his later books, including *The Winter of Our Discontent* and *Travels with Charley in Search of America* (1962), he pondered the future of American society. But Steinbeck was not just a political writer. In books such as *The Pearl* (1947) and *East of Eden* (1952) he explored even larger themes, tracing the consequences of jealousy and greed in human relationships.

He also pursued his interests in writing for the stage and films. He adapted several of his works for the theater and wrote others specifically for performance. Several of his works have been made into successful feature-length movies, including *The Grapes of Wrath, East of Eden,* and *Viva Zapata!* (1952), extending his influence into contemporary popular culture.

Steinbeck died in Sag Harbor, New York, in 1968. Six years earlier, in 1962, Steinbeck won the Nobel Prize for Literature, the most prestigious award in the world of letters. In his acceptance speech, he reaffirmed his belief in the role of the writer to help improve society. The award was a fitting finale to a long and meaningful career.

Richard Wright

Protest Novelist, Champion of Racial Equality
1908–1960

The son of a share-cropper who left his family and a schoolteacher who suffered a paralyzing illness, Richard Wright grew up in rural Mississippi, was raised by a series of family members, and even spent some time in an orphanage. As a writer, he channeled the frustrations of his impoverished childhood into some of the angriest literature of the twentieth century and, in the process, advanced the ideals of racial justice in the era before the Civil Rights movement.

Wright was born on September 4, 1908, in a region of Mississippi that was economically undeveloped and in a nation that was racially divided. Resentful of these limitations, he left home before graduating high school and lived the rest of his life in major cities, where segregation was less pronounced. First in Memphis, Tennessee, and then in Chicago, he completed his education on his own, developing an interest in literature while he held odd jobs. During the depression of the 1930s he worked for the Federal Writers' Project, a government agency designed to support writers until the economy improved. Sensitive to the growing rift between America's rich and poor, and aware that racial prejudice was inhibiting the economic survival of the African American community, he began to study alternative economic systems, including communism. After moving to New York in 1937, he published his first book, *Uncle Tom's Children* (1938), an award-winning collection of four novellas that combined his main obsessions: American race relations and the ideals of communist economics.

Dissatisfied with the tone of *Uncle Tom's Children*, which did not express the anger and horror he felt regarding the devastating effects of racial segregation, Wright changed his literary style during the next two years. He resolved to create as realistic an account of racial politics, and of growing up black in white

His crime seemed natural; he felt that all of his life had been leading to something like this. It was no longer a matter of dumb wonder as to what would happen to him and his black skin; he knew now.

∼ From *Native Son*

America, as had ever been published. He also decided to enrich his account with his new and increasingly radical political ideas. The result, his 1940 novel *Native Son*, was his masterpiece. Set in depression-era Chicago, *Native Son* is the story of Bigger Thomas, an African American teenager who accidentally kills a white girl and unsuccessfully attempts to hide his crime. Graphic in its depiction of violence and insightful in its portrayal of Bigger's psychology—particularly his anger, resentment, and fear of white people—*Native Son* shocked and horrified its audience. Nevertheless, the book captured the nation's attention and became a Book-of-the-Month selection and a best-seller, as well as the inspiration for a stage version and a 1950 movie. Subsequent fictional accounts of the African American experience, including Ralph Ellison's *Invisible Man*, built upon Wright's realistic vision, but *Native Son* remains a uniquely honest account of race relations in the years before the Civil Rights movement ended segregation.

Wright followed *Native Son*'s success with his influential and best-selling memoir, *Black Boy* (1945), which traced the persistence of racial hatred in America back to the era of slavery. Then, dissatisfied with the slow progress of civil rights in America, he moved to France in 1947. Having left the Communist Party five years earlier, Wright was still seeking a new intellectual basis for his work. He ultimately settled upon the European existentialist philosophy then flourishing in Paris. This philosophy, based on individual freedom, influenced his later fictional works including *The Outsider* (1953) and *The Long Dream* (1958) as well as his nonfiction, including *Black Power* (1954) and *American Hunger*, which was published in 1977. Although his primary concern would always be the plight of African Americans, he also reported on and supported the blossoming liberation movements on the African continent as former European colonies were gaining their independence.

Wright died of a heart attack on November 28, 1960. One of the most important American protest writers of the twentieth century, he was buried in Paris's Père Lachaise cemetery, a place famous as the final resting place of great poets. Born in humble circumstances and raised in some of the most isolated communities in the United States, Wright ultimately earned fame and respect around the world as a leading proponent of African and African American freedom.

Eudora Welty

Writer of the Deep South
1909–2001

E udora Welty's father was an insurance executive, and her mother was a genteel former schoolteacher who loved literature. According to most accounts, theirs was a close and loving family, and Welty did not suffer from want or severe hardship. Nor was she particularly isolated, though she spent most of her life in Jackson, Mississippi, where she was born on April 13, 1909. Her stories and novels, therefore, were not based on the difficulties of her personal life, unlike the fiction of so many of her peers. Instead, Welty believed that fiction could be a pure act of imagination. She used her imagination to create some of the sharpest, most humorous, and most elegant stories of the twentieth century. In the process, she became one of the most important writers of the American South.

Welty received an undergraduate education at Mississippi State College for Women and the University of Wisconsin, graduating in 1929. Considering a career in advertising, she attended Columbia University Graduate School of Business for a year. She returned to Jackson in 1931 when her father became gravely ill. Following his death, she worked for a local radio station, wrote society columns for the local newspaper, and wrote fiction. However, she did not publish her first story, "Death of a Traveling Salesman," until 1936.

In 1935 and 1936, she worked for the Works Progress Administration (WPA), a government program designed to create jobs during the Great Depression. Most notably, Welty explored Mississippi as a photographer, refining her skills as an observer.

> A thing is incredible, if ever, only after it is told—returned to the world it came out of. For their different reasons, he thought, neither of them would tell this (unless something was dragged out of them): that, strangers, they had ridden down in a strange land together and were getting safely back—by a slight margin, perhaps, but margin enough.
>
> ~ From "No Place for You, My Love"

By the early 1940s, fiction was occupying more of her time, and her short stories began appearing in major literary magazines such as *The New Yorker* and *The Atlantic Monthly*. Welty's first short-story collection, *A Curtain of Green* (1941), broadened her audience considerably. In stories such as "Why I Live at the P.O." and "A Worn Path"—which won a 1941 O. Henry Award as one of the best short stories of the year—she wrote about small-town southern life in a way that was both humorous and sympathetic to the odd characters she described. She followed this successful debut with two more volumes, *The Wide Net and Other Stories* (1943) and her first novella, *The Robber Bridegroom* (1942). She also began drafting her first novel, *Delta Wedding* (1946), the story of a wealthy, plantation-owning family preparing for a wedding.

During World War II, Welty lived in New York City and wrote about the war for *The New York Times Book Review*. To counter reader and editor prejudices against women correspondents, she was forced to assume a man's name, "Michael Ravenna," as her byline. Called home in the 1950s to care for her ailing mother and brothers, she wrote less frequently—her 1954 novel *The Ponder Heart* was her most noteworthy creation from this period—and only rarely commented on the social and political upheavals of the Civil Rights movement, which targeted southern cities like Jackson.

She resumed her career in earnest after her mother's death in 1966, and in 1972 she published her most celebrated work, the Pulitzer Prize-winning novel *The Optimist's Daughter*. Describing a southern woman's return to Mississippi to attend her father's funeral, it represented Welty's return to her most distinct subject matter: the peculiarities of family life in the Deep South.

In later years, Welty published essay and short-story collections as well as *One Writer's Beginnings* (1984), a celebrated memoir and an influential guide for writers. She also received countless honors, including a 1980 Medal of Freedom awarded by President Jimmy Carter and, in 1998, her own volume in the prestigious Library of America, a book collection that had until then included only the works of deceased writers.

Welty was ninety-two-years old when she died on July 23, 2001. Having witnessed nearly a century of American history from her home in Jackson, Mississippi, she provided a unique perspective on her country. Her rich, vivid stories of southern life were a much-needed contrast to the urban tales that have dominated modern American literature. In a wry, poetic style, she celebrated both the strengths and the weaknesses of her Mississippi neighbors. And she did so with incomparable grace.

Tennessee Williams

Southern Playwright, Theatrical Innovator
1911–1983

In his theatrical depictions of the American South, in his innovative and poetic approach to drama, and in his extraordinary popularity with theater and movie audiences, Tennessee Williams vastly expanded the role of the playwright in American culture. Sadly, the basis for his plays, and therefore the source of his professional success, was a life filled with hardship.

Thomas Lanier Williams was born in Columbus, Mississippi, in 1911. (He would not be known as "Tennessee" until 1938.) With his mother and his sister, Rose, he moved from town to town along the Mississippi River, following his grandfather, an Episcopal minister who frequently relocated. In 1918 he and his family reunited with his father and finally settled in St. Louis, where his father managed a shoe company. His parents' marriage was not a happy one, however, and both Williams children suffered the effects of their conflicts. Nevertheless, Thomas displayed considerable literary talent at a young age and began publishing short stories before his seventeenth birthday. He was accepted to the University of Missouri in 1929 but left during his junior year, when his father insisted that he take a job in the shoe business. Heartbroken and languishing in his father's factory, he would not graduate from college until 1938, when he earned his bachelor of arts degree from the University of Iowa.

> Oh, you weak, beautiful people who give up with such grace. What you need is someone to take hold of you—gently, with love, and hand your life back to you, like something gold you let go of—and I can!
>
> ∼ From *Cat on a Hot Tin Roof*

During the 1930s he wrote several plays that were produced by small southern theater companies. But his career did not begin in earnest until his first major effort, *Battle of Angels,* opened in Boston in 1940. And even after its production, he remained a largely unknown figure in dramatic circles. He labored for five more years before his work reached the center of American theater, Broadway in New York City. But once *The Glass Menagerie* opened on

Broadway (1945), Williams succeeded in dominating the American stage for the next twenty years.

Inspired by the unhappy relationship between Williams's own mother and sister, *The Glass Menagerie* capitalized on the technical possibilities of the modern stage as well as on Williams's poetic dialogue in representing the tensions between a disabled girl and the mother who tries to find her a boyfriend. The intensity of its emotion and its honest dissection of an American family impressed critics and audiences alike. It was awarded the New York Drama Critics' Award as the best play of 1945 and made Williams a celebrity.

He followed the success of *The Glass Menagerie* with two more popular successes, *Summer and Smoke* (1947) and his first Pulitzer Prize–winning play, *A Streetcar Named Desire*. Set in New Orleans and detailing the conflicts among a loud and volatile man, Stanley Kowalski; his weak-willed wife, Stella; and his genteel sister-in-law, Blanche DuBois, *A Streetcar Named Desire* was perhaps Williams's most insightful exploration of love and betrayal. It was also one of his most successful ventures into popular culture. The 1952 movie adaptation, starring Marlon Brando and Vivien Leigh, made Stanley one of the most recognizable characters in film history. It also made Williams one of the most sought-after screen writers. He subsequently wrote several screenplays, including the original script to the award-winning 1956 film *Baby Doll,* a portrait of a troubled marriage in the Deep South, and an adaptation of his second Pulitzer Prize–winning play, 1955's *Cat on a Hot Tin Roof.*

He wrote several more major plays in the late 1950s and early 1960s, including 1961's *The Night of the Iguana,* as well as novels and short stories, but difficulties in his personal life diminished his output in his later years. Williams never found the confidence and happiness to match his fame and wealth. Struggling with addictions to drugs and alcohol, haunted by his troubled past,

Marlon Brando and Vivien Leigh play Stanley Kowalski and Blanche Du Bois in the 1951 motion picture *A Streetcar Named Desire.*

and caring for his disabled sister, he produced less consistently in the 1960s and 1970s. By the time he died, in 1983, his fame was based almost entirely on his masterpieces of the late 1940s and the 1950s.

But during his twenty-year run as the preeminent voice in American theater, Tennessee Williams changed American literary culture. Like novelist William Faulkner, he reintroduced the American South to a literary and theatrical world focused on the big cities of California and the Northeast. Like Eugene O'Neill, he tested the limits of the stage and proved that Broadway could support more than its famous musicals and revues. And he examined American society through several literary forms—drama, film, short stories—leaving his mark on each.

Ralph Ellison

Writer Best Known for Invisible Man
1914–1994

On the strength of a single novel, *Invisible Man*, and a handful of essays and short stories, Ralph Ellison earned a reputation for being one of the finest and most insightful American writers of the twentieth century. In his detailed analyses of race relations and in his synthesis of a century of political and literary innovations, his small but brilliant body of work inspired generations of Americans of all races to think about their country in new ways.

> I am invisible, understand, simply because people refuse to see me. Like the bodiless heads you see sometimes in circus sideshows, it is as though I have been surrounded by mirrors of hard, distorting glass. When they approach me they see only my surroundings, themselves, or figments of their imagination—indeed, everything and anything except me.
>
> ～ From *Invisible Man*

Unlike many of the African American writers with whom he is often compared, Ellison was not a child of the rural South or the urban North. Born in 1914 in Oklahoma City, Oklahoma, he grew up in the Midwest at a time when that region featured the least racial hostility in the nation. He received a solid education and, despite his family's frequent financial difficulties, was able to enroll in 1933 at Tuskegee Institute in Alabama to study music. Tuskegee, the university founded in 1881 by Booker T. Washington, offered Ellison a new perspective on African American history and provided him with the setting for the first half of *Invisible Man*.

To support himself through his senior year, Ellison traveled to New York City in the summer of 1936 to work as a musician and study sculpture. He then returned to New York the following year to participate in the artistic culture that had been flourishing in the city since the Harlem Renaissance of the 1920s. Encouraged to pursue a literary career by eminent writers such as Langston Hughes and Richard Wright, Ellison found work with the Federal Writer's Project, a government program that supported writers during the Great Depression. He published several short stories during this period and prepared himself for his next job, an editorship at *The Negro Quarterly*. Although he was unwilling to enlist in the army, since it was still racially segregated, Ellison considered participation in World War II a patriotic duty. He therefore joined the merchant marine, in which he served until the end of the war.

Late in 1945, while on sick leave from the merchant marine, Ellison began the story that would become *Invisible Man*. During the next seven years, while his wife worked to support him, he wrote and revised the novel. By the time it was published, in 1952, it contained everything he knew about American race relations and everything he knew about American literature. Drawing on a variety of genres—from folk tales to science fiction—as well as the full tradition of African American literature, *Invisible Man* is the story of an unnamed black man determined to succeed in American society but, because of the complexity of racial interaction, continually prevented from achieving his goals. Frustrated by the limitations of southern society, he journeys to the North and finds work as a political agitator. In both regions, however, he is "invisible," ignored or stereotyped because of the color of his skin. *Invisible Man* won the 1953 National Book Award and was immediately considered among the best works in American literary history.

By 1955, Ellison had begun his second novel and settled into a career as a lecturer and creative-writing instructor at universities including Bard College, Rutgers University, and New York University. He also continued to accept awards at home and abroad for his ground-breaking work, including his influential volume of essays titled *Shadow and Act* (1964). In 1969 he even received the Medal of Honor, the most prestigious civilian honor in the nation. But despite frequent announcements that it would be finished shortly, Ellison could not complete his second novel. Then, in 1967, he lost much of his first draft in a house fire. He never recovered as a novelist. He published a second volume of essays in 1986, *Going to the Territory,* but when he died in 1994 he left behind an unedited manuscript of almost 2,000 pages. The manuscript was cut down to 350 pages and published in 1999 under the title *Juneteenth.* Many scholars, however, consider the novel a poor approximation of the one Ellison intended to write.

Ralph Ellison's crowning achievement, *Invisible Man,* was such an exceptionally rich and beautifully written account of life in America that it was immediately considered among the nation's very best works of fiction. It was also ambitious and important enough to sustain its writer's reputation through decades of relative silence. Perhaps it was so good that Ellison felt he could never fulfill the expectations it set for his second novel. For whatever reason, it stands as the sole monument to one of the century's truly gifted literary figures.

Saul Bellow

Novelist of Modern American Anxiety
1915–

Because he is the son of Russian Jews and often writes about Jewish-American characters, Saul Bellow is sometimes classified as a writer of ethnic fiction. However, while he frequently examines issues facing ethnic communities in the United States, Bellow is one of the most intellectually curious and expansive writers of the twentieth century. By combining his cultural concerns with a deep interest in literary and philosophic history, he has become

> Some people thought he was cracked and for a time he himself doubted that he was all there. But now, though he still behaved oddly, he felt confident, cheerful, clairvoyant, and strong. He had fallen under a spell and was writing letters to everyone under the sun.
>
> ∼ From *Herzog*

one of the most respected figures in world literature.

Bellow's parents were Russian immigrants who settled in Lachine, Quebec, a province of Canada, in 1913. Bellow was born two years later, into an environment that forced him to learn several languages: the English and French of his Canadian neighbors as well as the Yiddish and Hebrew of the Russian Jewish community. By the time his family moved to Chicago in 1924, he had already experienced a range of cultures and had an acute sense of the importance of words.

Graduating from the Chicago public-school system, he enrolled at the University of Chicago in 1933. Then he transferred to nearby Northwestern University, where he studied anthropology and sociology. In 1937 he attended one semester of graduate school at the University of Wisconsin before withdrawing to pursue his writing. By the beginning of 1938, he was determined to become a successful writer of fiction. Nevertheless, he taught school and worked as an editor on the Encyclopedia Britannica in order to earn a living. He also served in the U.S. merchant marine during the final years of World War II.

The war did not slow his literary progress, however. Before its end, Bellow published his first novel, *The Dangling Man* (1944), about the anxieties of a man waiting to be drafted into the military. And soon after the war, he published his second novel, *The Victim* (1947). Both novels were well received, but his third novel, *The Adventures of Augie March* (1953), was Bellow's first major contribution to American literature. An often-comic account of a young man's life in Chicago's Jewish community, the novel is loosely structured and skips from one "adventure" to the next in a literary style known as picaresque, a style based on random occurrences and one that Bellow would come to master.

The Adventures of Augie March won the 1954 National Book Award and introduced readers to Bellow's distinctive combination of realism, wit, and intellect. His 1959 novel, *Henderson the Rain King*, in which a dissatisfied Chicago businessman finds emotional fulfillment during a trip to Africa, continued his investigation of the American man at midcentury. And his 1964 novel, *Herzog*, the story of a Jewish intellectual contemplating suicide won another National Book Award. *Herzog* displays Bellow's extraordinary literary range by featuring picaresque elements, realistic depictions of modern relationships, and in the comic letters Herzog writes to famous thinkers from the past and present, a rich sense of intellectual history. By the time he won his third National Book Award, with his depiction of an American Holocaust survivor in *Mr. Sammler's Planet* (1970), Bellow was generally regarded as the leading American novelist of the postwar era.

He reached the pinnacle of his already-distinguished career in 1975, with the publication of *Humboldt's Gift*. The story of a successful novelist who wishes he were more like his friend Humboldt, an uncompromising but underachieving poet, *Humboldt's Gift* won the 1976 Pulitzer Prize and sealed Bellow's election, later that year, as winner of the Nobel Prize for literature.

Although he was in his mid-sixties when he won world literature's most prestigious award and appears to have achieved every goal an American writer can set for his work, Bellow refuses to slow down. Having taught at universities all over the world since the 1950s, he continues to hold teaching positions, including a long-standing appointment at Boston University. He has published several novels—including his most recent critical success, *Ravelstein* (2000), about a brilliant but troubled college professor—as well as several short-story and play collections and a book of essays, *It All Adds Up* (1994). And as a literary critic, he has participated in several of the major social debates of the age, although he does not cultivate the media attention or fame of contemporaries such as Norman Mailer and Philip Roth. Generally, Bellow relies on his novels—and his humorous, insightful, intelligent portraits of American men struggling to find their places in a complicated world—to speak for him.

Arthur Miller

Popular Playwright Best Known for Death of a Salesman
1915–

Arthur Miller's father, a Jewish immigrant and clothing manufacturer, suffered a series of financial setbacks during the 1930s. Like many other workers and entrepreneurs, he was ruined by the Great Depression. And like many other children who grew up during the depression, Miller never forgot the devastation of poverty. As a result of his family's experiences, he became convinced that people have a responsibility to assist each other and that all people,

> I'm gonna show you and everybody else that Willy Loman did not die in vain. He had a good dream. It's the only dream you can have—to come out number-one man. He fought it out here, and this is where I'm gonna win it for him.
>
> ～ From *Death of a Salesman*

no matter how poor or humble, deserve consideration and sympathy. The plays that ultimately made him famous broadcast these ideas throughout American culture, sometimes in spite of harsh public criticism.

An athletic boy who grew up in Brooklyn, Miller did not display a clear interest in intellectual pursuits until he entered the University of Michigan in 1934. While studying English and journalism, he became involved with the campus theatrical organization and won awards for his play *The Grass Still Grows.* After college he participated in President Franklin D. Roosevelt's New Deal, working on a variety of projects—including as a scriptwriter for radio programs—which were financed by the federal government to help combat the effects of the depression. Unable to fight in World War II because of a lingering sports injury, he continued to write during the war years. His first Broadway production, *The Man Who Had All the Luck* (1944), closed after six performances, but his first novel, a protest against anti-Semitism called *Focus* (1945), was a critical success.

Miller began to find his dramatic voice with his second Broadway play, *All My Sons,* which was first performed in 1947. Although it did not impress audiences, it won the New York Drama Critics' Circle Award that year and convinced many critics that Miller would rival Tennessee Williams as a premier playwright of the era. The story of a factory owner who manufactures defective airplane parts for the U.S. Air Force during World War II, *All My Sons* introduced Miller's most lasting themes: the corrosiveness of guilt, the inescapable nature of human responsibility, the tensions between fathers and sons. Always concerned with providing a moral, Miller created a play that was both philosophically important and accessible.

With his 1949 masterpiece, *Death of a Salesman,* he perfected his style and his message. In Willy Loman, a salesman whose fantasies about success ultimately disrupt his relationships at work and at home, Miller created perhaps the most famous character in American theater. By exploring the tragic potential of a common man's life, he also changed the public's expectations about appropriate subject matter for the stage. His sympathetic portrayal of the desperate and ineffectual Loman ushered in a new era of American plays about ordinary people. It also earned him the 1949 Pulitzer Prize. *Death of a Salesman* has been performed almost continuously since its debut, in countless revivals and in theaters around the world.

Miller's concern for the common American citizen was not always considered an admirable trait, however. In the early 1950s, while the United States and the Soviet Union were engaged in the hostilities of the cold war, the government sponsored investigations into the lives of people who may have been sympathetic to the Soviet Union's communist ideals. Protesting what he thought was a violation of American freedoms, Miller wrote *The Crucible* (1953), a play that compared the activities of the House of Representatives' Committee on Un-American Activities (known as HUAC) to the Salem witch trials of the seventeenth century and criticized them both as products of unreasonable paranoia. *The Crucible* won the 1953 Tony Award, but Miller was then called to testify before HUAC to defend his writings. Though Miller never supported the Soviet Union, he refused to cooperate with the committee, proclaiming his right to free speech, and was cited for contempt of Congress in 1956. HUAC's activities have since been condemned by most Americans, but Miller's defiance was dangerous in the mid-1950s and nearly cost him his livelihood.

After surviving HUAC's scrutiny, Miller continued to be an influential figure in literary circles. He also became a familiar figure in popular culture after he married actress Marilyn Monroe in 1956. He wrote the screenplay for Monroe's 1961 film, *The Misfits*, but their marriage did not last, and they were divorced that same year.

Miller's work since the mid-1960s hasn't received the same acclaim as his earlier plays. Critics, seeking more subtle representations of modern problems, have objected to his transparent plots and his insistence that each play convey a moral lesson. And audiences have responded to his plays, short stories, and memoirs with less fervor than they had in the 1940s and 1950s. Nevertheless, in the continual film and stage adaptations of his greatest works—*Death of a Salesman, All My Sons,* and *The Crucible*—Miller remains a vital force in American culture, a defender of basic freedoms and a champion of human dignity.

Robert Lowell

Confessional Poet of New England Society
1917–1977

obert Lowell's poetry was the intensely personal work of a man in conflict with himself and with the society into which he was born. Even when he discussed broad historic themes, he did so by first describing his own family's history as well as his responses to that history. Like Nathaniel Hawthorne, an earlier New England writer who influenced him greatly, Lowell transformed questions about his own past into questions about his

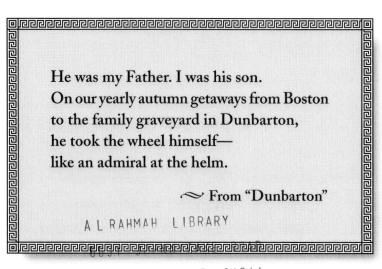

He was my Father. I was his son.
On our yearly autumn getaways from Boston
to the family graveyard in Dunbarton,
he took the wheel himself—
like an admiral at the helm.

From "Dunbarton"

nation's future. In the process, he helped to found a style of "confessional" poetry that greatly influenced American culture in the late twentieth century.

Born in Boston in 1917, Lowell descended from two powerful families with deep roots in New England history, the Lowells and the Winslows. Though this lineage was the source of wealth, privilege, and comfort, Lowell had mixed feelings about being a member of an elite society. To varying degrees, he would rebel against his family's expectations for the rest of his life.

His first rebellion was his decision, at an early age, to become a professional poet rather than to emulate his father, an officer in the U.S. Navy. In St. Mark's preparatory school and at Harvard University—with which the Lowell family had long been associated—he immersed himself in the history of poetry. Encouraged by poet and professor Allen Tate, he began experimenting with themes and forms. He left Harvard after his sophomore year, however, to study with an older poet, John Crowe Ransom, at Kenyon College in Ohio. Lowell excelled at Kenyon, graduating summa cum laude. More important, by studying in Ohio he proved his willingness to break with his family's traditions. In 1940, Lowell broke with another tradition, rejecting his family's Protestantism by converting to Roman Catholicism.

After graduating from Kenyan, Lowell studied for a year at Louisiana State University, married the writer Jean Stafford (the first of three wives), and moved into a house with Allen Tate and his wife, the novelist Caroline Gordon. In this literary atmosphere, he worked on his poetry and watched as the United States edged closer to involvement in World War II. When Japan bombed Pearl Harbor, Lowell tried to enlist in the army but was rejected because of his poor eyesight. In 1943, after two years of bloodshed in Europe and Asia, the army reversed its decision and drafted Lowell to fight. But by then, Lowell had come to see the war as a theater of senseless destruction, and he refused to report for duty, pleading a conscientious objector status. The U.S. government refused to grant him this status, however, and Lowell was imprisoned for several months.

Released from prison in 1944, he polished the poems for his first volume, *Land of Unlikeness* (1944), and set to work on the volume that would win the 1947 Pulitzer Prize, *Lord Weary's Castle*. This second collection was inspired by Lowell's religious faith as well as his obsession with New England history and was rich with the sense of loss that was characteristic of Lowell's best work.

After his father's death in 1950, Lowell published *The Mills of the Kavanaughs* (1951), a collection of poems that most critics rejected. Its failure inaugurated one of the most difficult periods in Lowell's life, during which he was frequently hospitalized for mental illness. As part of his therapy and recovery, Lowell wrote increasingly personal poems, explorations of his personal and family history that were later refined and broadened to comment on American society more generally. The result of this work was the formally innovative, personally revealing collection entitled *Life Studies* (1959), winner of the 1960 National Book Award. In the more famous poems of this cycle—"Waking in the Blue," his portrait of life in a psychiatric hospital, and "Skunk Hour," about the decline of his family's New England culture—Lowell mixed his personal anguish with social and historical observation in a way that critics dubbed "confessional." Following *Life Studies,* American artists in a variety of media, including poet Sylvia Plath, attempted to copy his honest, personal, even painful methods of self-expression.

In the 1960s and 1970s, Lowell devoted more of his time to his teaching at several American universities, and to political matters. In particular, he protested the escalating war in Vietnam. His poetry, such as his antiwar elegy "For the Union Dead," reflected his new political preoccupations. But he also turned his attention to the history of poetry itself; in a series of imitations, translations, and plays, Lowell adapted the works of famous writers to his own literary purposes. And he continued to write his unique brand of confessional poetry, including the verses collected in the Pulitzer Prize–winning *The Dolphin* (1973), until his death in 1977.

Robert Lowell combined the history of his family, the history of his country, and his own personal history—including his mental illness—in poems that addressed the major issues of his era. His honesty, even more than his obvious poetic skill, expanded the possibilities of self-expression in the 1950s and 1960s and changed American culture.

J. D. Salinger

Reclusive Author of The Catcher in the Rye
1919–

Although he has published one of the most popular novels of the twentieth century, Jerome David Salinger may be even more famous for what he has not published. At the height of his fame and influence in the early 1960s, Salinger withdrew almost entirely from public life. Since then, he has refused to release any more of his intense, compassionate stories, despite the pleadings of his fans.

> I'm the most terrific liar you ever saw in your life. It's awful. If I'm on my way to the store to buy a magazine, even, and somebody asks me where I'm going, I'm liable to say I'm going to the opera. It's terrible.
>
> ～ From *The Catcher in the Rye*

Born in Manhattan in 1919, Salinger grew up in a prosperous household and attended both public and private schools, including Valley Forge Military Academy in Wayne, Pennsylvania, from which he graduated in 1936. The following years were unsettled: He attended New York University for a short time, traveled to Europe with his father, enrolled for a semester at Ursinus College, and then attended Columbia University before leaving to pursue a writing career. Before being drafted to fight in World War II, he managed to place several short stories in popular magazines such as *Cosmopolitan* and *Esquire*.

While rising to the rank of sergeant in the Army Counter-Intelligence Corps and witnessing some of the heaviest fighting in Europe, Salinger continued to write stories for the magazines back home. When he returned from the war in 1946, he began placing his stories in *The New Yorker*, several of which were collected and published in his 1953 volume, *Nine Stories*. At the same time, he honed the novel he would also publish in 1953, *The Catcher in the Rye*.

The Catcher in the Rye is Salinger's primary achievement. The story of Holden Caulfield, a troubled, lonely sixteen-year-old boy who wanders New York City for two days, *Catcher* developed many of the themes Salinger had addressed in his stories, including the damage that adults knowingly and unknowingly do to children, the sadness of lost innocence, and the hypocrisies of the "phony" modern world. Wildly popular with readers—particularly teenagers—it has also become the subject of intense debate. Some school districts and libraries, objecting to its mature themes and its occasionally harsh language, have tried to ban it from their shelves.

Thirty-four-years old and already a national celebrity, Salinger appeared to be headed for a long and brilliant literary career. But without offering an explanation, he published sparingly in the late 1950s and early 1960s, focusing most of his work—in *Franny and Zooey* (1961) and 1963's *Raise High the Roof Beam, Carpenters* and *Seymour: An Introduction*—on the children of the Glass family, whom he first introduced in *Nine Stories*. And after 1963 he disappeared entirely from public view.

Living in seclusion in the New Hampshire countryside, Salinger has published only two stories since *Raise High the Roof Beam*, though there have been many suggestions that he continues to write. Salinger's sudden, unexplained withdrawal has contributed to his status as America's most mysterious living writer. Generations of readers who grew up with *The Catcher in the Rye* are still curious to see what he has written during the past forty years. But Salinger refuses to satisfy them. An intensely private man, he will not even agree to be interviewed.

Jack Kerouac

Novelist, Spokesman of the Beat Generation
1922–1969

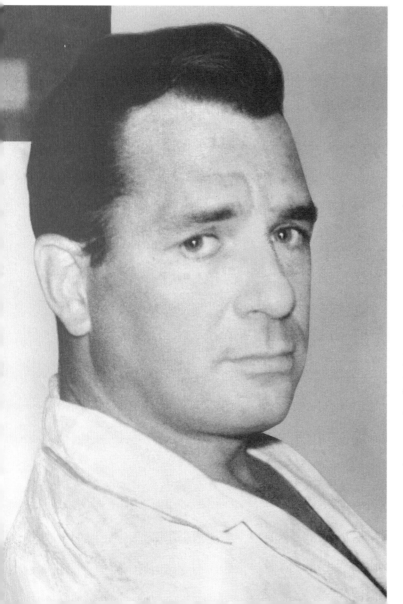

In the 1950s the United States was the wealthiest nation in the world. It was experiencing a baby boom, a technological revolution, and an expansion of suburban living. But to some, the country seemed a little too stable, a little too bland, and a little too boring. For this reason, Jack Kerouac's *On the Road* was the right novel at the right time.

In some ways, Kerouac lived the American dream. The son of French-Canadian immigrants, he was born in Lowell, Massachusetts, in 1922 and primarily spoke a dialect of French until he was six years old. Nevertheless, he succeeded as a high-school football player and earned scholarships to Horace Mann preparatory school and Columbia University, both in New York City. His future seemed bright. Yet Kerouac refused to follow the easy path to success. During his sophomore year at Columbia, he argued with his football coach, dropped out of school, and embarked on a life of adventure to rival that of his childhood hero, novelist Jack London.

> [T]he only people for me are the mad ones, the ones who are mad to live, mad to talk, mad to be saved, desirous of everything at the same time, the ones who never yawn or say a commonplace thing, but burn, burn, burn like spiders across the stars and in the middle you see the blue centerlight pop and everybody goes 'Awww!'
>
> ∿ From *On the Road*

By that time, the United States had entered World War II, so Kerouac joined the merchant marine. He wrote fiction during his years of service and devoted his entire life to writing when he returned to the States. In the summer of 1944, still living near the Columbia campus, he befriended several other young writers who would form the core of the group known as the beat generation, including Allen Ginsberg, William Burroughs, and Gregory Corso. The beats challenged mainstream American culture by living rebelliously, experimenting with drugs, and writing energetic, often explicit poetry and prose. In them, Kerouac found his inspiration and his literary support. But the beats also introduced Kerouac to a dangerous lifestyle, one that was occasionally violent and usually involved narcotics.

Soon after meeting Ginsberg, Burroughs, and the others, Kerouac fought with his parents, who were concerned about his career choices and still supporting him financially. After his father died in 1946, Kerouac wrote his first novel about the conflicts, *The Town and the City* (1950). It received fair reviews but sold poorly, and Kerouac began a desperate search for literary success.

He found his best subject in the person of Neal Cassady, a drifter from Denver and a friend of the beats. Cassady wrote fresh, animated letters that gave Kerouac new ideas about writing. Cassady also led him on long cross-country joyrides, showing him the country from new angles. From 1947 to 1949, Kerouac and Cassady hitchhiked and drove throughout the nation. Then, exhausted but anxious to write, Kerouac set to work on his masterpiece.

For years, he struggled with the book. Only when he taped together a long roll of blank typewriter pages, so that he could type without stopping, did he find the rhythm and voice for which he had been searching. The result was *On the Road,* a fictionalized account of his friendships with the beats and his travels with Cassady.

Fast-paced and action-packed, the book is an explosion of words and images, often bearing more of a resemblance to poetry—particularly Walt Whitman's—than prose. By design, it has very little plot. Sal Paradise (Kerouac's alter ego) and Dean Moriarity (the fictionalized Cassady) merely roam the countryside in an attempt to live as freely and happily as possible. Their search involves danger and great excesses, particularly in the scenes depicting drug use and alcohol abuse, and it does not always lead to happy endings. But it accomplishes the beats' primary goal: It reveals the creative energy beneath the calm surface of postwar America. It celebrates the spirit of rebellion that the nation had been trying to ignore.

After finishing *On the Road* in 1952, Kerouac completed a series of novels and poems that he would publish later, including *Doctor Sax, Mexico City Blues,* and *Book of Dreams. On the Road* was not accepted for publication until 1957, but when it was finally published it received rave reviews. The novel, with its romantic view of the wandering lifestyle, appealed to young audiences in particular, and Kerouac became an instant pop-culture hero. Soon America looked to him as the reluctant spokesman of the beat generation. Such acclaim proved to be a heavy burden.

Kerouac tried to build on the success of *On the Road* in later books including *Dharma Bums* (1958) and *Big Sur* (1962), reintroducing similar characters and themes. But he could not recapture the excitement or the success of *On the Road,* and he became frustrated with the public's constant demands. His later life was dominated by the alcohol and drug problems he developed during his experimental years with the beats. Alcoholism ultimately killed him in 1969, at the age of 47.

Kerouac paid a heavy price for the success of *On the Road,* both while he was gathering material for it and after it was published. Yet it remains one of the central works of the mid-twentieth century, a masterpiece of the beat generation, and one of the most entertaining explorations of freedom in American literature.

Kurt Vonnegut

Popular Satirist of Modern America
1922–

In the 1960s, Kurt Vonnegut's novels reached a small but enthusiastic audience of college-age readers. Mixing elements of science fiction and fantasy in stories that were often critical of American society, they were unusual works that fell outside of the literary mainstream. And Vonnegut himself remained a kind of cult figure, ignored by the mainstream culture, until he wrote about the most important event of his own life in his 1969 masterpiece, *Slaughterhouse-*

Five. Since then, he has been recognized as a unique writer in contemporary American literature, a writer who manages to amuse and provoke his readers simultaneously.

Vonnegut was born in 1922 in Indianapolis, Indiana. Although his parents began their lives in positions of wealth and influence—his mother's family owned a successful brewery; his father

> As a trafficker in climaxes and thrills and characterization and wonderful dialogue and suspense and confrontations, I had outlined the Dresden story many times. The best outline I ever made, or anyway the prettiest one, was on the back of a roll of wallpaper.
>
> ∾ From *Slaughterhouse-Five*

was a prominent architect—they never recovered from a series of financial setbacks during the Great Depression. Vonnegut attended local public schools, distinguished himself as an editor of his high-school newspaper, and aspired to become an architect like his father. But his father, still trying to mend his own business, encouraged him to study something more lucrative. Vonnegut therefore enrolled at Cornell University to study chemistry and biology. He displayed little talent in the sciences, however, and once again devoted most of his energy to the school newspaper.

Failing in most of his classes, he volunteered for the army in 1944 and studied in its Specialized Training Program. He reached the battlefields of World War II as an advance scout for an infantry battalion. While performing this dangerous duty during the Battle of the Bulge, he was captured by German soldiers and taken to the city of Dresden, where he was forced to live in a slaughterhouse. On February 13, 1945, as the city's air-raid sirens sounded, he and several other American prisoners raced to the slaughterhouse basement. From their safe position, they listened as American and British warplanes bombed the city. In the fire that followed the bombing, 135,000 of the city's residents were killed. As a survivor of the Dresden bombing, which he would describe in *Slaughterhouse-Five,* Vonnegut developed a unique awareness of life's absurdities and a deep revulsion to violence of any kind.

Returning to the United States later in 1945, he enrolled at the University of Chicago to study anthropology. He failed to earn his master's degree, however, when the faculty rejected his final research paper. He was more successful as a part-time reporter and, later, as a publicist for General Electric. While working for GE in 1950, he published his first short story in *Collier's* magazine. A year later he quit his job; moved to Cape Cod, Massachusetts; and attempted to build a career as a fiction writer. While continuing to publish short stories in popular magazines, he earned a living by teaching English in a local school. He also opened a car dealership. But these jobs became less important as he began publishing his novels.

With his first novel, a nightmare vision of a society dominated by machines entitled *Player Piano* (1952), Vonnegut seemed to align himself with popular science-fiction writers. Subsequent short-story collections reinforced this image, but he also displayed his abilities as a realist and a humorist in works such as the spy novel *Mother Night* (1962). When he finally combined science fiction with humor in *Cat's Cradle,* his 1963 fantasy about the end of the world, he earned recognition among a broader range of readers. By the time his next novel, *God Bless You, Mr. Rosewater,* was published in 1965, his work was being reviewed by all the major newspapers in America, and he was receiving teaching invitations from many academic institutions including the University of Iowa and, later, Harvard University.

For several years in the late 1960s, he worked on his fictionalized account of his Dresden experiences. The resulting novel, *Slaughterhouse-Five,* would become one of the key pacifist statements of the late twentieth century. By the time it was published in 1969, the United States was engaged in the Vietnam War, and Vonnegut's ironic approach and antiwar politics found a highly receptive audience. It quickly became the number-one book on the *New York Times* best-seller list and was followed by several other popular successes, including his 1973 farce *Breakfast of Champions* and his heartbreaking political satire *Slapstick* (1976). And even when critics tired of his manic, haphazard style, American audiences continued to clamor for his work. Though his production slowed in the 1980s and 1990s, his books often appeared on the best-seller lists, several of his stories were adapted for movies and television, and he became a more visible public figure.

In 1997, Vonnegut published what he claimed to be his final novel, *Timequake.* Nevertheless, he has released several collections of short works since. Having survived the bombing of Dresden, a series of personal tragedies, and decades of conflict with literary critics, he remains one of the most tenacious and feisty writers in American literature.

Norman Mailer

Novelist, "New Journalist," Public Figure
1923–

In the late twentieth century, American writers struggled to compete with television and the news media for national attention. Many tried to distance themselves from popular culture, hoping that they would appear more serious and more worthy of attention by standing apart from the American mainstream. But others used television and newspapers to promote their ideas and advance their careers. Of these latter writers, none achieved as much influence as Norman Mailer.

Mailer was born in Long Branch, New Jersey, but grew up in Brooklyn, New York. A graduate of a local public school, he attended Harvard University from 1939 to 1943, graduating with a degree in aeronautical engineering. While at Harvard, he

> For a moment he almost admitted that he had had very little or perhaps nothing at all to do with this victory, or indeed any victory—it had been accomplished by a random play of vulgar good luck hardened into a causal net of factors too large, too vague, for him to comprehend.
>
> ∼ From *The Naked and the Dead*

published several short stories in a campus literary journal, including "The Greatest Thing in the World," which also won *Story* magazine's 1941 award for the best short fiction of the year. Drafted into the army in early 1944, Mailer served as a rifleman on the Pacific front for the last two years of World War II. After his discharge in 1946, he studied at the Sorbonne in Paris and completed a sprawling novel, *The Naked and the Dead* (1948), based on his war experiences.

Chronicling a Marine assault on a Japanese-held island in the Philippines *The Naked and the Dead,* became an instant best-seller. Mailer, only twenty-five years old at the time, was heralded as the new genius of American literature. But he divided his energies among a variety of interests in the following years, working for a short time in Hollywood, editing *Dissent* magazine, and cofounding *The Village Voice,* a daring New York newspaper. As a result, his next two novels, *Barbary Shore* (1951) and *The Deer Park* (1955), were less polished and disappointed readers and critics alike.

The success of *The Naked and the Dead* may have misled Mailer's audience. Many of his early readers compared him to another American war novelist: Ernest Hemingway. But Mailer had something different in mind. Although he had written one of the finest novels about World War II, he did not aspire to be a conventional novelist. With the publication of *Advertisements for Myself* (1959), a diverse collection of his shorter work, he aligned himself with a very different style of writing known as new journalism.

In the kind of journalism found in most newspapers, reporters try to present the facts of their stories without including their own opinions. In contrast, new-journalism writers such as Norman Mailer deliberately included their opinions in their stories. As a result, new-journalism articles were often more argumentative, controversial, and politically motivated than conventional newspaper articles. Mailer published several major works in this style in the 1960s. The most important was *The Armies of the Night* (1968), his account of a massive antiwar demonstration that took place in Washington, D.C., in 1967. It won a National Book Award as well as a Pulitzer Prize.

Mailer capped a decade of intense political involvement with his 1969 campaign for mayor of New York. Although the campaign failed, it reinforced Mailer's status as a major figure in American culture. Hot-tempered but willing to suffer public criticism, he made many enemies in the 1970s. He was especially unpopular with the women of the feminist movement, of whom he was an outspoken critic. But in spite of his well-publicized feuds and his frequent television appearances, Mailer wrote steadily. In 1979 he produced another winner of the Pulitzer Prize: *The Executioner's Song*, a fictionalized biography of real-life killer Gary Gilmore.

Throughout his career, Mailer seemed most comfortable, and most successful, as a writer of long, complex, detailed works. *The Executioner's Song* and *The Naked and the Dead* each ran for almost a thousand pages. In the 1980s and 1990s, similar works occupied even more of Mailer's time. Although he published several acclaimed shorter works during these decades—including a murder mystery, *Tough Guys Don't Dance* (1984), and a fictionalized life of Jesus, *The Gospel According to the Son* (1997)—he staked his reputation on his epic novels: *Ancient Evenings* (1983), set in ancient Egypt, and *Harlot's Ghost* (1991), the first part of a projected series about the U.S. Central Intelligence Agency. Even if these novels failed to achieve the blockbuster success of *The Naked and the Dead*, they reinforced Mailer's reputation for as one of the most ambitious and fearless writers in American literature.

Whether he is promoting a new novel or running for public office, arguing with critics or leading a protest, Norman Mailer has been in the spotlight for more than fifty years. He has proven that good writers can prosper and even thrive in the age of television. And by maintaining both his literary stature and his celebrity, he remains one of the most visible and influential analysts of American society.

Flannery O'Connor

Writer Best Known for Ironic Stories of Southern Life
1925–1964

*P*hysically ill and, for the better part of her adult life, confined to her family's small dairy farm outside of Milledgeville, Georgia, Flannery O'Connor could not travel the world like other famous writers of her era. Instead she became a careful observer of the small-town life that surrounded her. And she made herself into one of the most astute writers of the American South in the years immediately following World War II.

Born in 1925 to a prominent Georgia family, O'Connor pursued her literary career through the university system. This was a relatively new approach for writers of the mid-twentieth century; earlier writers seldom learned fiction-writing skills as a part of their academic training. After graduating from the Georgia State College for Women, O'Connor enrolled in the graduate writing department at the University of Iowa. Then, after completing the requirements for her master's degree in 1947, she moved to the Yaddo writer's colony in upstate New York. At Yaddo, while living and working with other aspiring writers, she drafted her first novel, *Wise Blood* (1952).

> "You needn't act as if the world had come to an end," he said, "because it hasn't. From now on you've got to live in a new world and face a few realities for a change. Buck up," he said, "it won't kill you."
>
> ~ From *"Everything That Rises Must Converge"*

Before completing the novel, however, she began displaying symptoms of lupus, a hereditary disease of the immune system that had already killed her father. Weakened by the disease and uncertain of her future, she moved back to Milledgeville and into her mother's care. Venturing out only when her health permitted, O'Connor lived on the farm for the rest of her life, writing, painting, and caring for her pet peacocks. Eventually, she turned the limitations of her personal life into the material of her greatest fiction. By focusing her attention on the farm towns and villages that immediately surrounded her, she was able to draw profound conclusions about American society at large.

Novels that focus on the religious life of the Deep South, *Wise Blood* and *The Violent Bear It Away* (1960) displayed O'Connor's unique approach to her subject matter, which was by turns ironic, sarcastic, and loving. But it's her short stories that are primarily responsible for her reputation as a writer and critic of American culture. In her 1955 collection, *A Good Man Is Hard to Find,* as well as in *Everything That Rises Must Converge* (1965), a volume published after her death, she described the small-town South as the site of intense cultural conflict. Stories such as "Everything That Rises Must Converge" and "The Artificial Nigger" explored the tense relations between African Americans and whites at midcentury, predicting later developments in American race relations and the Civil Rights movement. Other stories such as "The River" and "A Temple of the Holy Ghost" investigated the changing significance of religion in the modern world. And violent, Gothic tales such as "A Good Man Is Hard to Find" and "Good Country People" revealed the dangers of pride and arrogance in human interaction.

Together, these stories provided a new and challenging portrait of American life at a time when the nation needed guidance. Following World War II, the United States had become one of the wealthiest and most powerful nations in the world. But O'Connor feared it had lost some of its religious and moral strength. She hoped that she would be able to restore some of that strength through her writing. To this end, she wrote stories that forced Americans to question themselves and to examine their behavior toward one another. Unwilling to abandon this mission, she continued writing through her long and painful illness, until her death in 1964.

Allen Ginsberg

Beat Poet, Activist
1926–1997

In their ecstatic poetry and prose, the beat writers of the 1950s rebelled against the restrictions of American society after World War II. Their literature was an influential antidote to the sober, colorless mainstream culture of the era. But once the initial shock of their techniques wore away, few of the beat writers continued to influence the national culture in important ways. Allen Ginsberg, a celebrated beat poet who participated in most of the major political and

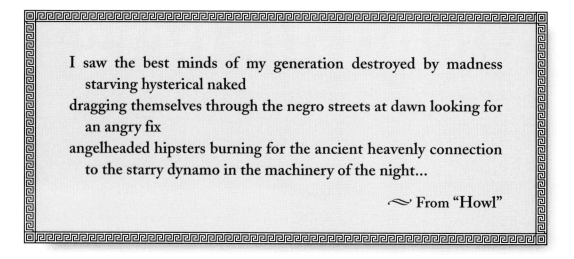

> I saw the best minds of my generation destroyed by madness
>   starving hysterical naked
> dragging themselves through the negro streets at dawn looking for
>   an angry fix
> angelheaded hipsters burning for the ancient heavenly connection
>   to the starry dynamo in the machinery of the night...
>
> ~ From "Howl"

social debates of the late twentieth century, was therefore unique.

Ginsberg was born in Newark, New Jersey, but grew up in the declining industrial town of Paterson. His father, Louis Ginsberg, was an English teacher and a poet; his mother, Naomi, was an active member of the American Communist Party who suffered from a variety of mental illnesses. Thus Ginsberg—a politically active but unstable poet who wrote about the spiritual decline of American society—owed much of his later poetry to the influences of his parents.

In 1941, when Ginsberg was a junior in high school, his mother suffered a psychological collapse and was hospitalized. In and out of institutions for the rest of her life, she would die fifteen years later while a patient in a Long Island, New York psychiatric hospital. His mother's deterioration would always haunt Ginsberg and eventually inspired some of his greatest poetry. But when he enrolled at Columbia University in 1943, he was emotionally shaken and had not yet considered poetry as an outlet for his feelings.

He began to change his mind after befriending a bedraggled group of aspiring writers—including Jack Kerouac and William Burroughs—who gathered near the Columbia campus and would soon be known as the Beat Generation. In their pleasure-seeking lifestyle and their faith in the power of literature to change the world, the beats suggested an alternative to the middle-class lifestyle that Ginsberg found stifling. But they also engaged in a number of self-destructive activities, including drug use, that would have long-term, negative consequences in Ginsberg's life.

In 1948, Ginsberg suffered a nervous breakdown and was hospitalized for eight months. After his release, he traveled to Mexico to continue his experimentation with hallucinogenic drugs. Then he settled in San Francisco, which was quickly replacing New York as the center of beat culture. Inspired by his friend Kerouac's recent poetic innovations, Ginsberg began work on a poem of his own, written in long, rhythmic lines that recalled the poetry of his literary hero, Walt Whitman. Entitled "Howl," the poem described the frustrations many young intellectuals felt in the years after World War II. Critical of the nation's materialistic culture and fascination with business, "Howl" proposed the free, spontaneous lifestyle of the beats as a solution to the nation's problems. It received such an enthusiastic response when Ginsberg began reading it in San Francisco clubs that it was soon the subject of a media frenzy. Almost overnight, Ginsberg joined Kerouac as a leading spokesman of the beat movement, and "Howl" became its most characteristic poem. When it was published in book form in 1956, however, the San Francisco police deemed it obscene and tried to halt its distribution. Their plan backfired. Ginsberg's publishers won the ensuing trial, and Ginsberg became even more famous as a defender of free speech.

In the following decades, Ginsberg continued to write rich and important poetry—including his second masterpiece, an elegy for his mother entitled *Kaddish* (1961). But his work as a social activist earned him an even wider audience than his poems. After spending two years in India studying Eastern religions, he returned to the United States in the mid-1960s as a committed pacifist who no longer depended on drugs for his inspiration. By the end of the decade, he was leading demonstrations to protest the Vietnam War and advocating environmentally responsible living.

In the later years of a career that had been characterized by literary and political revolt, Ginsberg, the poet once prosecuted as a menace to American society, became a respected figure in academic circles. He held several teaching positions in American colleges and continued to publish his mystical, intensely personal poems until his death in 1997.

With his electric poetry, he reached broader audiences than any of his peers. And with his social activism, he earned a position of cultural leadership during one of the more volatile periods in American history. Few twentieth-century writers occupied as prominent a place in American culture as Allen Ginsberg, and none remained in the public eye for as long.

Toni Morrison

African American Feminist Writer
1931–

As a book editor for the Random House publishing company during the 1960s and 1970s, Toni Morrison helped publish the works of influential African American writers and celebrities, including activist Angela Davis and boxer Muhammad Ali. In its own right, this work represented an important contribution to American culture. But the novels Morrison composed during this period, in her spare time and during her commute to and from her job,

> 124 was spiteful. Full of a baby's venom. The women in the house knew it and so did the children. For years each put up with the spite in his own way, but by 1873 Sethe and her daughter Denver were its only victims.
>
> ~ From *Beloved*

made her one of the most influential American writers of the late twentieth century.

Born Chloe Anthony Wofford on February 18, 1931, Morrison grew up in northern Ohio in an area rich with Civil War history and the memory of the Underground Railroad. She would prominently feature this region in her later writing.

Morrison was a talented student, and despite the limitations imposed upon African Americans and women in the era before Civil Rights, she flourished in the academic world. After graduating from Howard University in 1953, she received her master's degree in English from Cornell University in 1955, taught English at Texas Southern University, and returned to Howard as a teacher in 1957.

In 1964, after divorcing her husband, architect Harold Morrison, she moved to Syracuse, New York, where she supported her two children as a textbook editor for Random House. To unwind after her workday, she began writing stories of her own. She also edited and expanded a story she had written several years earlier, a tale about a black girl who prays that God will give her blue eyes. Soon this short story grew into a full-length novel. And by 1967, when she was promoted to senior editor in Random House's Manhattan offices (she was largely responsible for the African American authors on the company's roster), her manuscript was ready for publication.

The Bluest Eye was published in 1970, and Morrison was immediately celebrated as a unique voice in American literature. In her first novel, she exhibited an impressive insight into her characters' psychologies as well as a unique social and political perspective, combining the lessons of the Civil Rights movement with those of the re-energized feminist movement of the late 1960s and 1970s. With her next novels, *Sula* (1973) and *Song of Solomon* (1977), Morrison expanded the scope of her work and developed a dense, rhythmic style that drew on the modernist novels of William Faulkner as well as on the works of Harlem Renaissance writers such as Langston Hughes and Zora Neale Hurston. Critics consistently praised her work, and readers responded in kind. By the mid-1980s she was an acclaimed lecturer, a tenured professor at Princeton University, and a public figure respected as both an intellectual and a member of American popular culture.

Following the award-winning *Song of Solomon,* a novel about northern characters fleeing their southern pasts, Morrison published *Tar Baby* (1981) and completed her 1987 masterpiece, *Beloved.* Based on an actual incident that took place in 1851, when an escaped slave murdered her children instead of watching them return to slavery, *Beloved* is, like *Song of Solomon,* the story of a community haunted by its past. In Sethe, the guilt-ridden former slave; her angry daughter, Denver; and Beloved, the ghost of Sethe's murdered baby, Morrison presents a family forced to reckon with the violent legacy of slavery. In particular, she focuses on the harsh effects of slavery on African American women and the ways in which those women unite to survive their predicament. Written in a poetic prose that emphasizes the characters' psychological struggles, *Beloved* became an instant best-seller as well as a critical favorite, a rare combination in contemporary fiction. It earned the 1988 Pulitzer Prize for fiction and continues to be a defining text in American culture and a featured selection of college literature courses. In 1998 it became a major motion picture starring Oprah Winfrey.

In her subsequent novels, *Jazz* (1992) and *Paradise* (1998), Morrison has continued her lifelong exploration of African American culture and women's issues. In addition she has written dozens of essays on both literature and contemporary politics, some of which have been collected in *Playing in the Dark: Whiteness and the Literary Imagination* (1992), and has become a prominent commentator on American culture.

For her lyrical and incisive body of work, she won the 1993 Nobel Prize in literature. Having overcome the limits of prejudice and bigotry, Morrison became the eighth woman, and the first black woman, to win the most prestigious award in world letters.

Sylvia Plath

Poet of Personal Anguish
1932–1963

ew writers are the subject of as much controversy as Sylvia Plath. In a short career distinguished by her brilliant, disturbing poems as well as her psychological decline and self-destruction, she amassed a loyal audience and became a powerful symbol of the feminist movement that evolved during the early 1960s. Her life and her suicide in 1963, have therefore taken on an importance far beyond those of other twentieth century American poets.

> If the moon smiled, she would resemble you.
> You leave the same impression
> Of something beautiful, but annihilating.
>
> ∼ From "The Rival"

Plath was born in Boston in 1932. Her father, a German immigrant and a biology professor at Boston University, was a dominating presence in her early childhood. His death, when she was only ten years old, would later become the subject of many of her best poems. In its aftermath, Sylvia and her mother shared a strained relationship. Nonetheless, Plath excelled at school. She won several awards in high school, published her first short story in 1952 (in *Mademoiselle* magazine), and graduated summa cum laude from Smith College in 1955. She continued her education at the University of Cambridge, in England, as a Fulbright scholar. While in England, she met the British poet Ted Hughes, whom she married in 1956. Plath and Hughes had two children together, but their relationship was tumultuous from the start and would only become more destructive with time.

The couple returned to the United States in 1957, and Plath took a teaching job at Smith College in western Massachusetts. The following year she studied with Robert Lowell, the eminent American poet, before returning to England with Hughes. The result of her early experiments with her poetic voice was the 1960 volume *The Colossus.* The poems of *The Colossus* featured Plath's unsettling, often violent imagery, her impressive technical skill in an array of poetic forms, and her obsession with death. But they were less daring than the poems she would write during the following three years.

After the release of *The Colossus,* Plath's poetry reflected the deterioration of her marriage to Hughes as well as her morbid preoccupation with the death of her father. While they were unquestionably powerful expressions of sadness and anger—and perhaps her best work—poems such as "Lady Lazarus," which prefigured her own death; "Cut," based on her self-destructive impulses; and "Daddy," an assault on her father's memory, revealed a poet in distress. And as an examination of a woman's emotional breakdown during the restrictive era of the 1950s, her only novel, *The Bell Jar* (1963), reinforced this image of Plath as a wounded writer.

When she committed suicide in 1963, Plath's fans accused Hughes of cruel treatment and blamed him for her death. Several of the angry poems in her posthumously published masterpiece, *Ariel* (1965), were critical of marriage and seemed to support this theory. As a result many viewed Plath as a symbol of the mistreatment of all women in a male-dominated society. Literary critics and scholars continue to examine the effects of sexism, and of Hughes more particularly, on Plath's life and career.

Nevertheless, Hughes has helped to extend Plath's legacy. After her death, he oversaw the publication of her poetry, journals, letters, and fiction, including a wide variety of previously unreleased work. He also edited *The Collected Poems* (1981), a compilation of her poetry that won the 1982 Pulitzer Prize. As a result, Plath's popularity has not diminished in the forty years since her death. She remains the preeminent poet of the wounded and disenchanted in American literature.

John Updike

Writer Best Known for Stories of Suburban American
1932–

Before World War II, Americans lived in two basic environments: Some lived in towns and cities; others lived in rural regions. But after World War II, a third environment, the suburb, came to dominate American society. Dependent upon cities but featuring rural elements—open spaces, backyards, highways—the suburbs of the 1950s and 1960s represented a new mode of living. And the writer who described this new lifestyle most eloquently and memorably, and who helped Americans makes sense of the changes it inspired, was John Updike.

Updike was not a child of the suburbs, however. He was born in Shillington, Pennsylvania, in 1932 and grew up on a farm in nearby Plowville. Sickly as a youth, he depended on books for his enjoyment. At his mother's encouragement, he also began writing. This early education served him well; he graduated at the top of his high-school class and in 1950 received a scholarship to attend Harvard University. There, he joined the campus humor magazine, *The Harvard Lampoon,* and developed his skills as both a writer and a cartoonist. After graduating in 1954, he studied art for a year at the Ruskin School of Drawing and Fine Art in England before taking a job at the premier American literary magazine of the era, *The New Yorker.*

Updike had already published a short story in *The New Yorker* when he was hired to write reviews and articles for the magazine's humor section, called "The Talk of the Town." For two years he lived near *The New Yorker*'s main office in Manhattan. Then, in 1957, he left his full-time job as well as the big city and moved to Ipswich, Massachusetts. Living in a Boston suburb, free now to concentrate exclusively on his fiction, he began his writing career.

In 1958 he published his first book, a poetry collection entitled *The Carpentered Hen and Other Tame Creatures,* and in 1959 he published his first novel, *The*

> His hands lift of their own and he feels the wind on his ears even before, his heels hitting heavily on the pavement at first but with an effortless gathering out of a kind of sweet panic growing lighter and quicker and quieter, he runs. Ah: runs. Runs.
>
> ~ From *Rabbit, Run*

Poorhouse Fair. The story of an old-age home, *The Poorhouse Fair* received good reviews and paved the way for Updike's first major critical and popular success, his 1960 novel *Rabbit, Run.* In the novel's main character, Harry "Rabbit" Angstrom, a former high-school basketball player struggling to make sense of his restrictive adult life in the suburbs, Updike created his most enduring character. He would revisit Angstrom in three subsequent novels, tracing his development through three more decades of American history: *Rabbit Redux* in 1971, *Rabbit Is Rich* in 1981, and *Rabbit at Rest* in 1990. And in a short-story collection from 2000, *Licks of Love,* he would offer a postscript, "Rabbit Remembered." Both *Rabbit Is Rich* and *Rabbit at Rest* would win Pulitzer Prizes.

But Angstrom was only one of Updike's important contributions to American literature. In his 1963 National Book Award winner, *The Centaur,* he combined ancient mythology with contemporary life—as well as his own family history—to describe the relationship between a father and a son. In his controversial account of marital infidelity, *Couples* (1968), he explored the anger, hostility, and betrayal behind the perfect exterior of suburban living, a theme he revisited in his celebrated short stories about the Maple family, collected in the 1979 volume *Too Far to Go: The Maples Stories.* And in his memorable, humorous novels about the fictional writer Henry Bech—*Bech: A Book* (1970), *Bech Is Back* (1982), and *Bech at Bay* (1998)—he reflected on the profession of writing in modern American society.

Although these and other novels—including 1984's *The Witches of Eastwick,* which became a popular movie in 1987—made Updike a household name, he has pursued a variety of other literary interests including poetry, criticism, and sports-writing, and he remains a regular contributor to *The New Yorker.* Meanwhile, his 1995 novel about modern American spirituality, In the *Beauty of the Lilies,* has kept him at the forefront of American fiction.

Though less secretive than some of his contemporaries, Updike tries to keep his private life out of the popular press. His celebrity is therefore based almost entirely on his work: his honest accounts of suburban life, his talent for humorous observation, and his crystal-clear writing style. After four exceptionally productive decades of writing, during which he has produced twenty novels and a wide array of other works, he remains one of the nation's favorite and most important literary figures.

Philip Roth

Novelist of Jewish-American Life and American Identity
1933–

*P*hilip Roth began his literary career with his 1959 story collection, *Goodbye, Columbus.* It won the 1960 National Book Award. After successful debuts like Roth's, many writers fail to live up to the promise of their early work. But Roth has been able to maintain the intensity of his work for more than forty years. In fact, Roth's most recent novels, which typically assess American society through the lens of Jewish-

American culture, have been among his very best.

The son of an insurance agent from Newark, New Jersey, Roth grew up in a household deeply rooted in Jewish faith and culture. He attended the local public schools in his working-class neighborhood and then enrolled in college, first at nearby Rutgers University and then at Bucknell

> How pleased my teachers would be, I thought—reading, even here! But then this was not the first time, or the last, when, powerless before the uncertainty at hand, I looked to print to subjugate my fears and keep the world from coming apart.
>
> ~ From *Operation Shylock*

University in Pennsylvania. As a graduate student, he continued his studies in literature at the University of Chicago, from which he received a master's degree. Finally, after brief ventures into the military and the University of Chicago Ph.D. program, as well as his first efforts as an English teacher, he found a job as a film critic for *The New Republic,* an important political magazine, in 1959. This job allowed him to focus on his writing, and he published his first major fiction—the stories of *Goodbye, Columbus*—later that year.

During his years at Bucknell and the University of Chicago, Roth was able to step back from his Jewish heritage and analyze his experiences from a new perspective. He learned to compare his parents' ethnic culture to the mainstream American culture in a way that illuminated both cultures. The title story of *Goodbye, Columbus,* a novella in which a working-class Jewish man falls in love with an upper-class Jewish woman, was the first of his works to provide this unique perspective on American society. Set in Newark, it was also among the first to confuse readers, who could not decide if the book was fiction or a part of Roth's autobiography.

His fourth novel, *Portnoy's Complaint* (1969), confused the boundaries between fact and fiction even more. Constructed as a confession to a psychiatrist, *Portnoy's Complaint* is the story of a Jewish-American man, Alexander Portnoy, who seeks happiness in a series of failed relationships with women. Notorious for its candid humor and explicit language, it offended as many readers as it intrigued. Leaders of the Jewish community were particularly outraged by its criticisms of Jewish life. Nevertheless—or perhaps because of the scandal—*Portnoy's Complaint* was the best-seller of the year and made Roth a noteworthy public figure.

Roth first responded to his newfound celebrity by frustrating his readers' expectations. In political satires such as *Our Gang* (1971) and literary satires such as *The Great American Novel* (1973), he varied his writing style and tried to avoid repeating the successful formula of *Portnoy's Complaint*. But with 1974's *My Life as a Man*, Roth adopted what became his most characteristic strategy: He made his own celebrity a subject of his novel. In describing the life of a fictional writer, Nathan Zuckerman, *My Life as a Man* invited readers to question whether it was also describing Roth's life, whether "Zuckerman" was simply another name for Roth. Subsequent Zuckerman novels, including *Zuckerman Unbound* (1981), continued to fascinate readers with these questions as they explored the difference between fiction and reality in the modern world. Roth finally reached the logical conclusion of these themes in his 1993 novel *Operation Shylock*, in which a character named "Philip Roth" meets another character named "Philip Roth" while researching a court case in Israel.

Roth retired from teaching in 1992 after holding professorial positions at several universities—including Iowa State, Princeton, the University of Pennsylvania, and Hunter College—since the 1960s. His retirement was followed by a resurgence in his fiction, as he began exploring broader cultural themes. His most recent novels, including three books that have been called his American Trilogy—*American Pastoral* (1997), *I Married a Communist* (1998), and *The Human Stain* (2000)—have reintroduced the character of Nathan Zuckerman but are less obsessed with ideas of fact and fiction and are more engaged in questions about American society and politics in the late twentieth century.

Having won three National Book Awards (for *Goodbye, Columbus; Sabbath's Theater* [1995]; and *American Pastoral*), a Pulitzer Prize (for *American Pastoral*), and a variety of other awards, Roth remains a key figure in American literature. Though famous for his depictions of Jewish-American life, he has proven to be one of the most ambitious writers of the twentieth century, able to blend interests in ethnic culture, American society, and the nature of fiction itself into a unique body of work.

Don DeLillo

Postmodern Novelist of the Information Age
1936–

America became an increasingly complicated place in the final decades of the twentieth century. Faster modes of transportation and new modes of communication connected people, cultures, and ideas in unexpected ways. To describe the complexities and unfamiliar features of this information age, writers of the 1970s, 1980s, and 1990s, led by Thomas Pynchon, devised new literary styles, often labeled "postmodern" by scholars and critics.

Chief among these writers was Don DeLillo, whose dense, ambitious novels addressed the political, economic, and cultural forces that dominate the modern world.

DeLillo was born in the Bronx section of New York in 1936. The son of Italian immigrants, he grew up in an Italian-American neighborhood that preserved many of its old-world traditions. After initiating his own literary education as an eighteen-year-old, by spending his summer reading the novels of Ernest Hemingway and William Faulkner, he enrolled at nearby Fordham University. Never a dedicated student, he nevertheless developed a diverse array of interests, including an appreciation for modern art and jazz, and graduated in 1958. For the next five years, he worked as a copywriter for an ad agency. Though he disliked the job, it revealed to him the inner workings of American business and the media, subjects he would soon examine in his fiction.

In 1964, DeLillo quit his full-time advertising job. Uncertain about his next profession, he wrote advertising copy when he needed to make money and wrote short stories to pass the time. He did not decide to write fiction full-time until he had completed half of his first novel, *Americana,* the story of a filmmaker's journey through the United States. *Americana* was published to mixed reviews in 1971. It was quickly followed by *End Zone* (1972), which

> This is the language of waves and radiation, or how the dead speak to the living. And this is where we wait together, regardless of age, our carts stocked with brightly colored goods. A slowly moving line, satisfying, giving us time to glance at the tabloids in the racks.
>
> ∼ From *White Noise*

received better reviews, and a rock-and-roll novel called *Great Jones Street* (1973), which puzzled readers and critics alike. In an era of less-ambitious literary works, such as Raymond Carver's stories about working-class people, DeLillo's sweeping portraits of American life seemed not only unfashionable but false.

Increasingly confident in his abilities, however, DeLillo continued to base his novels on profound philosophic, political, and literary ideas. *Ratner's Star* (1976) addressed the complexities of contemporary science, *Players* (1977) explored the inner workings of Wall Street, and *Running Dog* (1978) criticized the American fascination with violence.

DeLillo lived in Greece for three years in the early 1980s, during which he wrote *The Names* (1982), a novel about Middle Eastern terrorism. His time away from the United States gave him a fresh perspective on his native land, a perspective he turned into his first masterpiece, *White Noise* (1985). A satirical story about the life of a college professor in a community saturated by the entertainment media (the "white noise" of American culture) and threatened by environmental disaster, *White Noise* won the 1985 National Book Award and is now considered one of the best postmodern novels in American literature.

DeLillo followed the success of *White Noise* with his most politically informed and controversial book, *Libra* (1988), a fictionalized account of the life of Lee Harvey Oswald, the assassin of President John F. Kennedy. Then came *Mao II* (1991), another study of terrorism in the global society. And in 1997 he published what many critics consider to be his crowning achievement, *Underworld,* an 800-page work that blends fictional characters with actual historical events and spans the second half of the twentieth century.

What all of DeLillo's novels have in common, and what makes them "postmodern," is their focus on the systems—political, scientific, cultural—that make up contemporary life. His characters are influenced in profound ways by political events, television shows, scientific discoveries, natural disasters, and even sporting events. Because DeLillo is sensitive to these influences, he has become a valued commentator on American life. However, he remains an intensely private person and rarely agrees to sit for interviews. For the most part, he speaks only through his intelligent and challenging novels.

Raymond Carver

Master of the Modern Short Story
1938–1988

In his understated short stories and poems, Raymond Carver captured the feelings of limitation and frustration that pervaded American society in the late 1960s and the 1970s. An unlikely candidate for literary fame, he wrote about the lonely and dispossessed with a unique insight and compassion, attracting a large audience for his work. But what truly set his best stories apart, and what made his personal life noteworthy, was the way he was able to turn desperation into hope.

Born in Clatskanie, Oregon, in 1938, Carver was not raised in a literary environment. His father was a sawmill worker who suffered from alcoholism. His mother worked odd jobs to support her troubled family. Moving from town to town along the Pacific Northwest, they rarely stayed in one place. As a result, Carver became an intensely shy young man. He attended high school in Yakima, Washington and appeared more interested in hunting and fishing than in academics. In 1957 he married his sixteen-year-old high-school girlfriend and began raising a family. Before he was twenty-two years old, Carver was supporting two children.

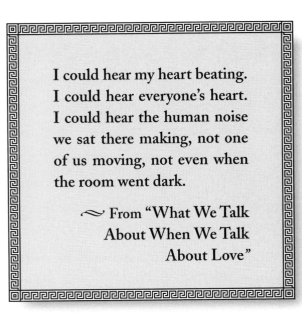

I could hear my heart beating. I could hear everyone's heart. I could hear the human noise we sat there making, not one of us moving, not even when the room went dark.

From "What We Talk About When We Talk About Love"

At first he held a number of jobs involving manual labor. But in 1958, while living in California, he attended a fiction-writing class at Chico State College. His professor, fiction writer John Gardner, encouraged him to develop his talent. Determined to earn his living as a writer, Carver enrolled at Humboldt State College, earning his bachelor's degree in 1963. He then pursued a master's degree in fine arts at University of Iowa, graduating in 1967. At the same time, he began publishing poems and writing fiction, including his first published short story, "Will You Please Be Quiet, Please?"

Carver's graduate degree allowed him to earn a living as a writing teacher at colleges and universities around the country. But he was not a particularly reliable employee. Absolutely devoted to his writing and fighting alcoholism, for which he was occasionally hospitalized, he frequently quit his teaching jobs. He remained a prolific writer, however, publishing two volumes of poetry, *Near Klamath* (1968) and *Winter Insomnia* (1970), as well as two celebrated short-story collections, *Put Yourself in My Shoes* (1974) and *Will You Please Be Quiet, Please?* (1976) within ten years of receiving his master's degree.

Carver's poems were irregular in form and based almost entirely on the simple rhythms of everyday speech. Typically they focused on fleeting moments of insight, episodes in people's lives during which they come to some important realization about themselves and the world around them. By emphasizing these moments, also known as epiphanies, Carver's poems resembled his short stories. Often set in the Northwest, his stories described working people struggling to salvage their relationships in a depressed and often hopeless era. Without explicit reference to political or economic issues, they expressed the sadness and disappointment that many Americans felt during the Vietnam War and the economic decline of the 1970s. But what truly made Carver's stories unique was his clear, concise, deceptively simple style. He inspired a host of imitators in the 1980s, but few have captured the power of his precise sentences.

Carver stopped drinking in 1977 and renewed his commitment to writing. The results, collections entitled *What We Talk About When We Talk About Love* (1981) and *Cathedral* (1983), displayed a new optimism. In stories such as "A Small, Good Thing" and "Cathedral," his characters began to find solace and comfort in human interaction. His poems, collected in volumes including *Where Water Comes Together with Other Water* (1985) and *Ultramarine* (1986), revealed a similar hopefulness. And Carver found happiness in his personal life as well, particularly in his 1988 marriage to poet Tess Gallagher (he divorced his first wife in 1977).

Tragically, Carver died later in 1988 after a battle with lung cancer. Since his death, Gallagher has released previously unpublished poems and short stories as well as two volumes of his collected works: a story collection entitled *Where I'm Calling From* (1988) and a poem collection entitled *All of Us* (1998). Carver therefore remains a dominant presence in contemporary American literature.

For Further Reading

Biographies

Anderson, Madelyn Klein. *Edgar Allan Poe: A Mystery.* Danbury, Conn.: Franklin Watts, 1993.

Burke, Kathleen. *Louisa May Alcott.* Broomall, Penn.: Chelsea House, 1988.

Coil, Suzanne M. *Harriett Beecher Stowe.* Danbury, Conn.: Franklin Watts, 1993.

Douglass, Frederick. *Frederick Douglass: In His Own Words.* Edited by Milton Meltzer. Orlando, Fla.: Harcourt, 1995.

Dyer, Daniel. *Jack London: A Biography.* New York: Scholastic, 1997.

Gates, Henry Louis and K.A. Appiah, ed. *Zora Neale Hurston: Critical Perspectives Past and Present.* New York: Amistad Press, 1993.

Hardy, P. Stephen and Sheila Jackson Hardy. *Extraordinary People of the Harlem Renaissance.* Danbury, Conn.: Children's Press, 2000.

Keene, Anne T. *Willa Cather.* Messner, 1995.

Kramer, Barbara. *Toni Morrison: Nobel Prize-Winning Author.* Berkeley Heights, NJ: Enslow, 1996.

Leach, William. *Edith Wharton.* Broomall, Penn.: Chelsea House, 1987.

Meltzer, Milton. *Benjamin Franklin: The New American.* Danbury, Conn.: Franklin Watts, 1989.

———. *Mark Twain; A Writer's Life.* Danbury, Conn.: Franklin Watts, 1985.

Osofsky, Audrey. *Free to Dream: The Making of a Poet, Langston Hughes.* New York: Lothrop Lee & Shepard, 1996.

Reef, Catherine. *Walt Whitman.* Clarion, 1995.

Stefoff, Rebecca. *Herman Melville.* Messner: 1994.

Tessitore, John. *F. Scott Fitzgerald: The American Dreamer.* Danbury, Conn.: Franklin Watts, 2001.

_____. *John Steinbeck: A Writer's Life.* Danbury, Conn.: FranklinWatts, 2001.

_____. *The Hunt and the Feast: A Life of Ernest Hemingway.* Danbury, Conn.: FranklinWatts, 1996.

Anthologies

Andrews, William L., Minrose C. Gwin, Trudier Harris, and Fred Hobson, eds. *The Literature of the American South: A Norton Anthology.* New York: W.W. Norton & Co., 1997.

Charters, Anne, ed. *The Portable Beat Reader.* New York: Penguin, 1992.

Delbanco, Andrew, ed. *Writing New England: An Anthology From the Puritans to the Present.* Cambridge, Mass.: Belknap Press, 2001.

Ford, Richard, ed. *The Granta Book of the American Short Story.* New York: Penguin, 1993.

_____. *The Granta Book of the American Long Story.* New York: Penguin, 2003.

Kilcup, Karen L., ed. *Nineteenth Century American Women Writers: An Anthology.* Oxford, U.K.: Blackwell Publishers, 1997.

Lewis, David L., ed. *The Portable Harlem Renaissance Reader.* New York: Penguin, 1995.

Lyon, Thomas J. ed. *The Literary West: An Anthology of Western American Literature.* New York: Oxford University Press, 1999.

Negri, Paul, ed. *Civil War Poetry: An Anthology.* New York: Dover, 1997.

Web Sites

Pegasos: A Literature Related Resource Site

http://www.kirjasto.sci.fi/

A site designed by scholars from Finland, it features detailed profiles of hundreds of writers from around the world.

The American Academy of Poets

http://www.poets.org/

This site includes essays on poetry, biographies of more than 450 poets, text of more than 1,250 poems, and RealAudio recordings of one hundred poems read by their authors or other poets.

The Nobel e-Museum

http://www.nobel.se/literature/laureates/

The official website of the Nobel Foundation, the organization that awards the Nobel Prize for Literature, the e-Museum includes biographies of all laureates as well as the texts of the press releases announcing the awards, presentation speeches, and the award-winners' Nobel lectures.

The Nobel Prize Internet Archive

http://almaz.com/nobel/nobel.html

This highly interactive site features links to news articles and websites about each laureate. It is not affiliated with the Nobel Foundation.

In addition to the general sites listed above, scholars and fans have launched individual websites devoted to almost every writer featured in this book. Many—especially those affiliated with American universities—provide interesting and useful accounts of the writers' lives and works.

Index

Numbers in *italics* represent illustrations.

Photo Credits

Photographs © 2004: AP/Wide World Photos: cover bottom right, 246, 253, 260, 264, 268; Art Resource, NY/National Portrait Gallery, Smithsonian Institution, Washington, DC: 58; Beinecke Rare Book and Manuscript Library, Yale Collection of American Literature: cover center right, 194; Corbis Images: cover bottom left, cover center left, cover top right, back cover top left, back cover top center, back cover bottom center, 19, 30, 38, 47, 50, 56, 62, 68, 82, 86, 89, 98, 105, 111, 114, 118, 122, 125, 136, 146, 158, 170, 174, 187, 198, 206, 213, 231, 234, 257 (Bettmann), 242 (Christopher Felver), 54 (Hulton-Deutsch Collection), 249 (S.I.N.), 227 (Oscar White), 42, 64, 92, 94, 109, 154, 162, 166, 182, 202; Getty Images/New York Times Co.: 272 (Chester Higgins Jr.), 129; Hulton|Archive/Getty Images: cover top left, back cover top right, back cover bottom left, 22, 26, 34, 79, 133, 138, 178, 210, 223, 238; Library of Congress: 66, 142 (via SODA), 72, 150; Magnum Photos: 215 (Bob Adelman), 191 (Marc Riboud), 219 (Ferdinando Scianna); Photo Researchers, NY/Library of Congress: 75; Superstock, Inc.: 14; The Kate Chopin House: back cover bottom right, 102.

Copyright extends to corresponding image on Contents page.

About the Author

John Tessitore is currently pursuing his doctorate in American Studies at Boston University. He has written young adult biographies of Ernest Hemingway, Muhammad Ali, Kofi Annan, John Steinbeck, and F. Scott Fitzgerald.